gumbo

LOUISIANA TRUE books tell the stories of the state's iconic places, traditions, foods, and objects. Each book centers on one element of Louisiana's culture, unpacking the myths, misconceptions, and historical realities behind everything that makes our state unique, from aboveground cemeteries to zydeco.

PREVIOUS BOOKS IN THE SERIES:

Mardi Gras Beads

Brown Pelican

Mardi Gras Indians

Po'Boy

gumbo

JONATHAN OLIVIER

Louisiana State University Press
Baton Rouge

Published by Louisiana State University Press
lsupress.org

LSU Press Paperback Original
Manufactured in the United States
First printing

Designer: Barbara Neely Bourgoyne
Typeface: Source Sans Variable
Printer and binder: Integrated Books International (IBI)

Portions of chapter 3 first appeared in "The Pot Thickens," *Bitter Southerner* (2021), and are reprinted here with permission of the *Bitter Southerner.*

Cover illustration: The Speckled Palate/Erin Parker (modified)

Library of Congress Cataloging-in-Publication Data
Names: Olivier, Jonathan, author.
Title: Gumbo / Jonathan Olivier.
Description: Baton Rouge : Louisiana State University Press, [2024] | Series: Louisiana true | Includes bibliographical references.
Identifiers: LCCN 2023046282 (print) | LCCN 2023046283 (ebook) | ISBN 978-0-8071-8201-7 (paperback) | ISBN 978-0-8071-8242-0 (pdf) | ISBN 978-0-8071-8241-3 (epub)
Subjects: LCSH: Gumbo (Soup)—History.
Classification: LCC TX757 .O46 2024 (print) | LCC TX757 (ebook) | DDC 641.81/3—dc23/eng/20231204
LC record available at https://lccn.loc.gov/2023046282
LC ebook record available at https://lccn.loc.gov/2023046283

contents

acknowledgments

Only a few years ago, I knew little of gumbo or its history—it was simply a food that I grew up with and that practically everyone I knew adored. That all changed after meeting culture bearer Dusty Fuqua, who is, in large part, the reason this book exists. Dusty has worked for more than a decade to highlight the Indigenous tradition of making filé from sassafras leaves. I first met him virtually back in 2019 or so, following him on Instagram to learn more about his sassafras foraging trips in the Kisatchie National Forest in Louisiana. A freelance journalist at the time, I thought he would make for a compelling profile for an article. So, in 2021, I followed him on a harvest day so that I could write about sassafras and its importance to gumbo's history for the *Bitter Southerner.* My article, titled "The Pot Thickens," led to an inquiry from LSU Press about writing this book. Thanks again, Dusty, for highlighting such an important Louisiana tradition. I also want to thank Josina Guess with the *Bitter Southerner* for assigning my article and for her editorial guidance, and Rory Doyle, the talented photographer who made the story come together.

I'd also like to recognize the late John Oswald Colson, Dusty's mentor, who was a Creole from Cane River and a respected culture bearer. Colson, also known as the Filé Man, learned the art of making filé from his family and continued the practice throughout his life. Although we never had the pleasure of meeting, Colson inspired Dusty and many other Louisianans to continue a beloved tradition that began with Native Americans like the Choctaw.

gumbo

Known around the world as Louisiana's flavorful soup, gumbo is a complex dish that originated after the convergence of Native Americans, Africans, and Europeans in the region. (Photo by Rory Doyle)

1

The Gumbo Family Tree

In the collective vernacular of Louisiana, cold fronts usher in gumbo weather. Just the slightest hint of a cool snap, which might send temperatures marginally below 70 degrees, functions as a sort of culinary call to arms. The weapons of choice? The biggest stew pot available, a long-handled stirring spoon, and a lot of time to kill. What results after those many hours of stirring, watching, and more stirring is a hearty dish that has, in many ways, come to represent Louisiana cuisine. What actually constitutes a gumbo, though, is much more complicated. While the dish is widely accepted as a sort of thick soup full of an assortment of ingredients, what those ingredients are and how they're arranged is, for some folks, nothing short of sacrosanct. And Louisianans are just as willing to go to battle over what goes in the gumbo pot.

Often, gumbo opinions have been informed by regional or family traditions that are hardened into deeply held convictions. Put more simply: it comes down to how Mom or Mawmaw cook it. I was schooled in the ways of gumbo by my mom, who grew up in Arnaudville, a small, historically French-speaking community in south Louisiana. She always cooked with chicken on the bone, smoked sausage, and thin strips of smoked pork called *tasso.* She used roux that she cooked in the microwave, adding it only after the onions, bell peppers, and meat had browned and the broth was simmering. We never had okra, although the blame was on my brothers and me and our finicky tastes. Our rice was always white, steamed to perfection in a dated, olive Hitachi rice cooker that's a staple in many Cajun and Creole homes. Sometimes we added a pinch of ground sassafras leaves, called *filé,* right in our bowls, but most times we didn't. Ritz crackers were a must, used for scooping rice and morsels of meat. If we were lucky, we also got potato salad on the side.

For me, Mom's gumbo is gumbo.

Yet, her version of the dish and our rituals surrounding it are much different compared to other folks across Louisiana—or even across the street. A friend of mine whom I grew up with starts his gumbo by cooking a roux together with onions, bell peppers, and celery. A New Orleans friend skips the roux entirely, using tomatoes, okra, and oysters. A few vegetarians I know, who can't imagine going without gumbo, cook with greens and vegan sausage, but they still use a roux for that hearty taste. As New Orleans chef Isaac Toups told me, "Gumbo is different in New Orleans. Gumbo is different in Acadiana. Gumbo is different at my house. Gumbo is different in my restaurants when I do make it . . . Gumbo means something different to everybody else because everybody takes a different interpretation on it."

Gumbo was born out of a similar spirit of experimentation and regional variation, anchored by a fusion of ethnicities that spanned the globe. It was only possible due to European colonization in North America, enslaved West Africans and Black Creoles, and contact with Native Americans. In the seventeenth century, the French were the first Europeans to colonize the region that now encompasses Louisiana. Although the colony of La Louisiane spanned the Mississippi River Valley to the Canadian border, the bulk of the settlement was concentrated in the coastal region in New Orleans and the surrounding areas, reaching westward to Lafayette, Opelousas, and Natchitoches, and northward up the Mississippi to Baton Rouge and Pointe Coupee Parish. The French brought with them enslaved people from West Africa, notably from the Senegambia region. Native Americans had lived in this region along the Gulf coast for thousands of years, people like the Chitimacha, Atakapa-Ishak, Avoyels, Appalousa, Houma and Choctaw. In 1762, Spain took control of the colony of Louisiana, while groups such as Germans, Acadians, and Haitians continued to settle in its coastal region. France regained control of the colony in 1801, only to sell it to the United States in 1803, which led to its statehood in 1812. These groups of people swapped foodways, language, and music to create a new culture thanks to this concentrated diversity in south Louisiana. In *French, Cajun, Creole, Houma: A Primer on Francophone Louisiana,* historian Carl A. Brasseaux described Louisiana's cultural landscape as "one of the most complex, if not the most complex, in rural North America." With so many differing voices from far-flung places in the world, something unique was bound to have been birthed. At the same time, this complex past means that gumbo's history is as robust as its broth and often as messy as the kitchen after stewing a pot of it.

Since gumbo is a by-product of adaptation and experimentation, it has never really fit neatly into one single recipe, nor has it conformed to claims of authenticity—but that hasn't stopped people from trying. It's unclear what makes a gumbo authentic to begin with. Is it the roux, the hearty mixture of fat and flour cooked to almost-burnt perfection? Some might say it's the okra, an ingredient found in gumbo ever since it was first cooked in New Orleans. Maybe it's the smoked sausage that has been seared just right in a cast-iron pot. It might be all these things or none of them. There has always been a myriad of ways to make a gumbo that vary by region, cook, and personal preference. When the gumbo was prepared makes a difference, too. In the eighteenth century, some folks made gumbo with cabbage. An 1803 memoir by Frenchman Pierre Clément de Laussat mentioned a gumbo with sea turtles—not exactly a gumbo staple these days.

Instead of considering gumbo's authenticity, looking at it as a dynamic dish with many tastes, smells, and ingredients better encapsulates what it is and always has been. In order to tell the story of gumbo, the ingredients can do much of the talking, in all of their many flavors and forms from across the centuries. Food, like art or language, is versatile and typically contextual, meaning something to group of people at a certain time, in a certain place. Therefore, it's important to include the many hands that were involved in the creation of the dish, too, in order to form a better understanding of who contributed to gumbo and why.

* * *

Gumbo has morphed into a larger-than-life cultural creation that is now representative of Louisiana's unique character. The state's cultural mélange is often referred to as a gumbo, a mix of different elements from around the world. Although the dish means something different to most everyone, there's a special level of reverence reserved for gumbo. In 2004, it was declared Louisiana's state dish. At graduations, weddings, Christmas, or lazy Sundays during football season, you'll find gumbo on the table. It's a dish worthy of disposable bowls and plastic spoons, while it's also capable of serving as the star of a party complete with fancy porcelain dinnerware.

A contemporary gumbo can be comprised of a host of elements that, more or less, are commonly stewed together. In *Stir the Pot: The History of Cajun Cuisine,* the authors offered that there are three types of modern gumbo: poultry, seafood, and a sort of quasi-vegetarian version called *gombo z'herbes.* Okra and roux are often present in each one, or sometimes filé, while individual tastes govern how much. The poultry gumbos feature a variety of fowl, like duck, quail, chicken, or dove, along with sausage to add flavor. Typically, sausage doesn't appear in seafood gumbos, which are usually comprised of crabs, oysters, or shrimp. Some folks will add tomatoes, while others consider that sacrilege. A *gombo z'herbes* contains greens, aromatic herbs, and often ham or sausage—although during Lent, many of Louisiana's Catholics will forgo the pork. Many gumbos fall outside of these classifications, made with ingredients like rabbits and squirrels, even eggs or hot dogs.

While it's tempting, as a Louisianan, to look at gumbo as a dish born solely in the Bayou State and completely unique to this region, there's more to that story. In fact, Louisiana gumbo shares a few qualities with many dishes. For starters, gumbo is a simple one-pot soup. Soups and stews containing a collection of different fare are a cornerstone of culinary history, with archaeological evidence suggesting that early humans were making one-pot soups as far back as twenty-five thousand years ago. Folklorist John Laudun, a professor at the University of Louisiana at Lafayette (ULL), explained in an essay in *Acadians and Cajuns: The Politics and Culture of French Minorities in North America* that "Cajuns and Creoles are not alone in possessing the secret of gumbo in the New World. There are . . . gumbos in the Carolinas and guigumbos in Puerto Rico." Laudun, who has studied gumbo and its origins, pointed out that "neither the name nor the idea for the dish itself is unique to the area."

One needs only to look at a map of the African diaspora to understand Laudun's point. Many peoples in West Africa, a region targeted by the transatlantic slave trade, had for generations stewed down okra to be served with rice—okra is native to the continent. Essentially, in every place in the Western Hemisphere that we find people with ancestral ties to Africa, from South America to the Caribbean to North America, there are gumbo-like dishes that are served with okra.

In the United States, soups that look awfully close to gumbo are easy to find. The Chesapeake Bay, with its long seafood traditions and history of enslaved Africans, is home to Maryland crab soup, which has been served with okra. Then there's the Carolina gumbo that Laudun mentioned, also known as Lowcountry okra soup, which is a seafood stew with okra, tomatoes, and rice. This dish was birthed by the Gullah Geechee people of the lower Atlantic coast, who are descendants of Africans. Writing for the *New York Times,* Samin Nosrat noted, "Okra soup is not necessarily Louisiana-style gumbo, thick with roux and rich with sausage and shrimp. Rather, it's a simple, wholesome dish that, like the best Gullah Geechee cooking, emphasizes the freshness of its ingredients."

Nosrat made a good point in singling out a few items unique to Louisiana's gumbo in order to differentiate it. Even though this Creole stew might share common qualities with soups and gumbo equivalents throughout the African diaspora, the evolution of Louisiana's gumbo is still a pretty unique one, which resulted after generations of experimentation by cooks with origins from around the world, as well as Indigenous contributions from right here in North America. Gumbo comes from West and Central Africans, Native Americans like the Choctaw, and Europeans like Spaniards, Germans, and the French. Along the way, other immigrants made their mark, like Italians.

In order to make the origins of Louisiana gumbo clearer, I like to think of it existing on a family tree. At the base of the tree, the story starts with the initial ancestors: West African okra stew and Choctaw soups. Many peoples from West Africa were enslaved in New Orleans starting in 1719, and they arrived with okra seeds. This tropical plant did well in Louisiana's warm climate, and Black Creoles continued to stew down okra as their ancestors had in Africa. This dish was often paired with rice. At the beginning of the nineteenth century, thousands of newly arrived Haitians of African descent from Saint-Domingue added to the stew's evolution. This group brought with them an affinity for tomatoes and spices like cayenne, which became ingrained in New Orleans Creole cuisine. Meanwhile, the Choctaw, an Indigenous group native to the Southeast, had long cooked soups of all sorts that contained finely ground sassafras leaves, called *filé* by the French. These soups contained plants like poke leaves, corn, wild game, or shellfish. After the Spanish made contact with the Choctaw in the sixteenth century, French colonizers allied with them in the early eighteenth century. It's at this time that the French likely encountered soups with filé. It wasn't long before filé and gumbo became practically synonymous.

What okra and filé have in common is that they both can turn a watery soup into a gelatinous porridge while adding flavor to it, too. The conventional wisdom goes that by putting two thickeners in the pot, the broth would be rendered too thick and not soupy enough. Doctrine dictated early on that okra and filé were to serve as the base of the family tree's initial, principal gumbos: okra gumbo, or *gombo févi* in French, and *gombo filé,* or gumbo made with ground sassafras. Cynthia LeJeune Nobles, in a chapter of *New Orleans Cuisine: Fourteen Signature Dishes and Their Histories,* called this "gumbo's golden rule—never add okra and filé in the same pot."

These two gumbos were unalike the contemporary dish in both taste and appearance. Early on, who knows if anyone even called the dish "a gumbo." Eventually, someone did—who and when, we'll probably never know. The dish first enters the historical record more than forty years after French colonization, in 1764, on a court document detailing a deposition from enslaved Africans. Historian Gwendolyn Midlo Hall found the document, handwritten in French, that included the interrogation of a fifty-year-old enslaved woman named Comba in New Orleans. Comba was being questioned about a runaway enslaved person, Louis, who had allegedly stolen clothes and a pig. During the deposition, she was asked if she had given Louis and a group of enslaved peoples *un gombeau.* Hall declared that this referred to the dish, not the okra pod, which is also *gombo* in French.

The interrogation occurred in September, so assuming the alleged crime occurred not long before, this gumbo likely had okra, since the plant would have been in season throughout the summer. Comba probably had the stewed okra with rice, too. What else could have appeared, though, is uncertain. It's not until twenty years later that we get an idea of how the branches of the gumbo family tree might have looked. More than a decade ago, historian Shane K. Bernard was on a search to uncover information about the origins of gumbo using primary, historical documents from the eighteenth century. In his quest, he uncovered a 1784 work by the French botanist François Rozier called *Observations sur la physique, sur l'histoire naturelle et sur les arts.* The work mentioned a host of flora and fauna from across North America, including a part on sassafras. In a section titled "Observations sur le sassafras, arbre de l'Amérique," by P. de la Coudrenière, Bernard came across one of the earliest-known accounts of gumbo ingredients: "The Creoles of Louisiana love it so passionately, that they cannot eat any other soup than this one made with broth, pepper, sassafras, and corn or rice cooked in water. Admittedly, this soup is much healthier and better tasting than our soups of bread. They make gumbo with all kinds of meat, poultry and fish. They also make it with shrimp and crawfish. That of cabbage is less esteemed; it is eaten, as is that of shrimp, in the evening, and is often served instead of dinner" [Bernard's translation from French].

While not exactly a recipe, this early list of ingredients provides insight into what comprised an array of late eighteenth-century gumbos. It seems that gumbo pots were then, like now, cauldrons of experimentation. What went in these soups likely depended on the cook, time of year, and ingredient availability. A few items that Coudrenière listed stand as outliers that would never appear these days, like the fish and cabbage. Corn, too, isn't found in gumbo pots today, yet it's listed alongside rice as a starch option to bring the dish together. While Africans cultivated rice and used it quite often, corn was a readily available option, too. Having cultivated corn for eons, Native Americans taught Europeans its many uses.

Hardly sixty years had passed since the French founded New Orleans, and already quite a few branches had appeared on the gumbo tree—cabbage gumbo, shrimp gumbo, gumbo with poultry—although it's unclear how these iterations were stewed together. One of the earliest gumbo recipes in print is Mary Randolph's version, which she included in her 1824 work *The Virginia House-wife,* the first cookbook printed in the South and one of the most well-known cookbooks of the nineteenth century. Randolph wrote, "Gather young pods of ochra, wash them clean, and put them in a pan with a little water, salt and pepper, stew them till tender, and serve them with melted butter." Randolph's gumbo isn't necessarily Louisiana gumbo. She associated it instead with the West Indies, as she named it "Gumbo—A West India Dish." At this time, the West Indies—the Greater and Lesser Antilles of the Caribbean today—were home to many enslaved people of African descent who were, like in Louisiana, stewing down okra. Randolph, born to a slave-owning family in Virginia, would have been well acquainted with enslaved people of the Commonwealth and the food they cooked.

Other recipes of the early nineteenth century also associated okra gumbo with the West Indies. In the United States, it isn't until later on that gumbo starts to become tied solely to Louisiana, and New Orleans, specifically. And from then on, the Louisiana version of the dish becomes the de facto gumbo in the nation's collective consciousness, a Creole creation all on its own. As a journalist boldly claimed in an 1877 article in the *Morning Star and Catholic Messenger,* published in New Orleans, "They have cotton and rice and tobacco elsewhere, they have grain and pork and silks, they have imports and exports, palaces and fountains, they have art and science, talent, beauty and accomplishment elsewhere as well as here, but they have not gumbo. Gumbo is in New Orleans only. It originated here, it expanded and grew to perfection here."

In 1840, Eliza Leslie's *Directions for Cookery, in Its Various Branches* listed a gumbo recipe that she described as "a favourite New Orleans dish," which contained okra, tomatoes, and onions. *The Carolina Housewife,* written by Sarah Rutledge and published in 1847, included a recipe called "New Orleans Gumbo" that featured "two spoonsful of pulverized sassafras-leaves." The fact that filé makes an appearance is further evidence that gumbo ingredients from Louisiana had found their way outside of the region. A decade later, ground sassafras also appears in another of Leslie's works, *Miss Leslie's New Cookery Book,* published in 1857, and she called the powder *filet.* Her recipe for "filet gumbo" included browning fowl and onions in lard before letting it simmer for three hours: "Then stir into it two heaped tea-spoonfuls of sassafras powder. Afterwards, let it stew five or six minutes longer, and then send it to table in a deep dish; having a dish of boiled rice to be eaten with it by those who like rice."

Rice had long been on the gumbo family tree. Most rice produced in the United States in the eighteenth and early nineteenth centuries came from South Carolina, North Carolina, and Georgia. The grain was also locally grown in Louisiana by Africans who had experience cultivating it, notably those from Senegambia. Other groups employed the technique for growing what is called "providence rice," according to Chan Lee in his dissertation about the history of rice in Louisiana. This subsistence, small-scale technique involved someone tossing rice grains in a natural wet spot, often without irrigation, and letting nature do the work—if the area stayed wet and the rice grew, there would be some to harvest. This was the most common way to grow rice in Louisiana until 1850, when production started to grow along the Mississippi River thanks to steam-powered pumps. At this time, around 87 percent of the rice production came from farms hugging the Mississippi and nearby bayous. In 1882, the Southern Pacific Railroad, which spanned the prairies of southwest Louisiana, had been completed, attracting midwestern farmers who tried their hand at rice farming. David Abbott, who arrived in Acadia Parish, Louisiana, from Michigan, developed an irrigation method using buckets and a one-half horsepower engine to gather water from a nearby bayou in order to irrigate his fields. His method was imitated by others in the region. By 1894, Abbott had dug the first large-scale canal in southwest Louisiana specifically for rice irrigation, which reached nearly four miles long. According to Henry C. Dethloff in "Rice Revolution in the Southwest," in the thirty-year period between 1880 and 1910, "rice production increased from a few thousand bushels of 'providence rice' used for home consumption, to a twenty-million-bushel commercial crop valued at approximately $16 million." Rice, becoming so ubiquitous in Louisiana, became inextricably tied to local cuisine—and gumbo specifically.

Up to this point in the late nineteenth century, the gumbo family tree has been constructed using recipes from outside of Louisiana, mostly from white, anglophone women who were more familiar with the cuisine of the East Coast than that of the Gulf Coast. After the Civil War, recipes from Louisiana cooks, as well as from African Americans, start appearing in newspapers and books. One of the earliest gumbo recipes from a Louisianan of color was published in 1873 by Alexander Dimitry, a New Orleans–born professor and writer who was the first person of color to attend Georgetown University, as well as to serve as a United States ambassador, a role he held starting in 1859. His filé gumbo rendition was featured in *Le Meschacébé,* a French-language newspaper from the Crescent City. The recipe includes chicken, oysters, and ham, which are stewed with onions, parsley, and celery. He advised using a "half pod of cayenne pepper, or a sufficient quantity of the ground, to give pungency." The soup is thickened with only a heaping tablespoon of filé after the pot was removed from the fire, and it was to be served with either rice or bread.

Dimitry's use of onions, celery, and a pepper is reminiscent of what today is commonly called in heavily Catholic Louisiana "the holy trinity"—onions, bell peppers, and celery—referring to the Christian doctrine of the existence of God, his son, and the Holy Spirit. The moniker was popularized in the 1970s. Typically, the trinity is sautéed in lard or oil in one of the first steps of gumbo preparation. Similar variations of the trinity have existed for centuries and go by all sorts of names. The Spanish are prolific users of *sofrito,* an aromatic mix of garlic, tomatoes, bell peppers, and hot peppers—the latter three of which are New World vegetables that arrived in the Mediterranean with conquistadores' plunders—while the French were accustomed to starting several dishes by sautéing a *mirepoix,* a mixture of onions, celery, and carrots. The Germans' version is called *suppengrün,* consisting of carrots, celery root, and leeks, with the occasional onion or parsnip. In West Africa, many dishes begin with a combination of tomatoes, chili peppers, and onions. Like all of gumbo's parts, the trinity's vegetables arrived on the Creole table by the hands of many different cooks, from West Africans, the French, Spanish, and Germans. The trinity isn't only used in gumbo but also in Louisiana's many dishes like étouffée, rice and gravy served with a choice of meat, red beans and rice, and jambalaya. The trinity is so pervasive that Guidry's Cajun Foods, based in Arnaudville, sells containers of precut trinity onions, celery, and bell peppers with a smattering of garlic, parsley, and green onions.

By 1885, the gumbo family tree gets more structured, and it resembles modern gumbo in many ways. Lafcadio Hearn published *La Cuisine Creole,* offering a more complete picture of Louisiana gumbo that is not too different from today's versions. In total, there were eight gumbo recipes in the collection, which is regarded as the first book that is focused specifically on New Orleans cuisine. Hearn, who was a journalist, author, and translator, collected New Orleans recipes not as a Creole himself, but as a sort of ethnographer and folklorist. He was born on the Greek island of Leucadia and found his way to New Orleans in 1877 after stints around Europe, New York City, and Cincinnati. While in the Crescent City, Hearn became fascinated with the local culture, which included language and foodways. Hearn collected stories, songs, and local sayings that resulted in newspaper essays and eventually a book published in 1885 called *Gombo Zhebes: Little Dictionary of Creole Proverbs.*

In his cookbook, Hearn listed options such as "Simple Okra Gumbo," a mix of meat, onions, spices, and okra. Another, similar to Dimitry's, featured chicken, oysters, and ham. Hearn even offered a Lenten option, not surprising for heavily Catholic Louisiana, that called for shrimp, crabs, or codfish in lieu of beef, poultry, or pork. Many of Hearn's gumbo recipes also featured filé. In the recipe "Gombo Filee with Oysters, No. 2," Hearn began by advising the cook to fry "a tablespoonful of flour in a tablespoonful of lard. Let it brown slowly so as not to scorch." Although he doesn't call this mixture a roux, that's exactly what he was describing. In one of his gumbo recipes, Hearn also appears to be describing the importance of roux in gumbo: "All gombo should be thickened with a little flour—browned if preferred—and stirred in just before adding water."

Roux entered Louisiana cuisine by way of the French. Pierre de Lune, a cook for the French king, is credited as roux's creator sometime in the fourteenth century. By the seventeenth century, cooks were routinely using roux, sometimes called *farine frit,* by mixing flour with lard and, later, butter. In Louisiana, lard was the most readily available fat, which was derived from bears in the early days and then, eventually, pigs. The word *roux* means "russet brown," referring to the color of the mixture of flour and fat that, when cooked slowly and long enough, turns from resembling peanut butter to milk chocolate or, depending on who's cooking it, dark chocolate. Adding it to gumbo not only thickens the broth but produces a rich flavor that's become synonymous with gumbo's heartiness.

Roux wasn't always on the gumbo family tree, though. It doesn't appear in most recipes from the early nineteenth century—many people opted for okra or ground sassafras to thicken the broth. Roux began to appear in the pot alongside either filé or okra, breaking the initial golden rule of using only one thickener. It wasn't until the twentieth century that roux and gumbo became inseparable, according to Nobles in *New Orleans Cuisine,* with mentions in cookbooks like *Dixie Meals* in 1934, and *New Orleans Cookbook* in 1940. Eventually, Opelousas-born chef Paul Prudhomme's stardom helped catapult the dish—with its roux base—to fame. In one of his nationally syndicated segments called "The Magic of Chef Paul," Prudhomme stirred briskly in a pot, demonstrating the steps to make a roux: "Making a roux . . . it's one of those Louisiana things that works with everything. It just makes things better." He goes on to declare that when "making gumbos and étouffées, you got to have it." Roux had been inextricably tied to gumbo, and Louisiana cuisine in general, a trend that continues today. Lake Charles's tourism department described roux as "the basis" of gumbo. A recipe from the Food52 website asserted that "a proper gumbo—thick, rich, affirming of hunger and soul—calls for a proper roux." And then there's the popular adage, "first, you make a roux," which is meant to act as a guide to anyone hoping to cook up a pot of hearty gumbo.

Today, there seems to be no gumbo without a mixing of flour and fat. Yet, despite the popularity of roux in gumbo, sometimes its importance can be overstated. Folklorist John Laudun explained in his essay about gumbo that "the conventional wisdom among the literati about gumbo is that 'first you make a roux.' A more careful survey of gumbo preparation reveals that this is simply not true . . . [T]he first thing you do in any gumbo is brown something. What you brown, how you brown it, and how much of that browning reveals itself in the final dish varies across regions, cooks, and kinds of gumbos. Browning is the one aesthetic impulse that transcends all gumbos." Laudun called browning "the gumbo engine."

Laudun noted that browning was a junction for the three folk cookeries—the Native Americans, French, and Africans. Apparently, Indigenous people browned grains or acorn powder while the French and Africans were already browning meat. Laudun even goes on to suggest that the Indigenous practice of browning cereal grains could be the origin of the Creole dark roux. The original French roux, after all, would have never been seared to such colors.

Today, some gumbos contain no roux at all, only browned meat and vegetables like onions, with okra or filé to thicken the broth. Others feature a "dry" roux, or one made with only flour but no oil or fat, where the cook stirs flour on a hot pan until it's browned. In parishes near Opelousas, the holy trinity is browned in one pot while fat and flour are cooked in another. Only after the meat has sizzled for long enough, and as the vegetables and the broth are simmering, is the roux added. In parts of coastal Louisiana, the roux is often browned along with the vegetables, which some credit with creating a more robust flavor.

Gumbo's flavor is often further enhanced today by pork. Pigs, which are not native to North America, were introduced to the continent in the sixteenth century by the Spanish conquistador Hernando de Soto. In *New Orleans Cuisine,* Nobles noted that when the Spanish took control of the Louisiana colony in 1762, their affinity for pork ensured it remained a part of Creole cuisine for decades. Various cookbooks call for ham in gumbo up until the 1950s, when the trend started to fade. While smoked sausage or andouille are considered modern pork staples of gumbo, they don't often appear on early branches of the gumbo family tree. In *The Picayune's Creole Cook Book,* originally published in 1901, of the nine gumbo recipes listed, sausage appears only in the cabbage gumbo recipe. These smoked links became more popular in gumbo as the twentieth century progressed. Louisiana-style andouille sausage is a gift from the Germans who settled about twenty-five miles upriver from New Orleans in 1721. These people of Swiss-German ancestry were led to what was eventually called the "German Coast" by Karl Friedrich D'Arensbourg. Here, they quickly earned a reputation as hard workers, supplying not only New Orleans with crops, but lands as far away as France and Haiti, then known as the colony of Saint-Domingue. Their booming production was made possible by enslaved people, some African and some Native American. By 1762, there were more than 530 enslaved people spread across 186 German Coast farms. Just two years later, the first French-speaking Acadians began arriving after having been exiled by the British from their homeland of Nova Scotia in 1755. A group of these Acadians settled north of the Germans, in what would be called the "Acadian Coast." Ken Wells, in his memoir *Gumbo Life: Tales from the Roux Bayou,* noted that these newly arrived exiles quickly took to new methods of cooking: "The Germans took in the Acadians and marriage with Cajun women was commonplace . . . The Germans clearly taught the Cajuns the art of sausage-making and the evolution of the modern andouille sausage, now a gumbo staple, is one result of this bicultural accommodation."

In the twentieth century, the gumbo family tree continued to grow, although not as rapidly. Some gumbo versions fell out of favor, like the cabbage gumbo or ham gumbo, but many others remained favorites, like chicken and sausage gumbo, *gombo z'herbes,* or crab gumbo. In many of these iterations, you can still find okra, filé, the holy trinity, and rice. As has been the case throughout gumbo's history, new branches are still being added to the tree as people experiment—but folks still just call it gumbo. This singular moniker maybe has less to do with the ingredients and more to do with the spirit that the dish embodies. Despite the differences in all of these versions, what they have in common is they arrive from many far-flung places around the world.

Of course, there are other ingredients that crop up in gumbo pots that haven't been mentioned in detail. What's been missing in this broad retracing of gumbo history are some of the most important parts: the stories of okra and filé. These two gumbo versions are at the base of the soupy family tree for a reason—without them, gumbo wouldn't exist. Much can be explained by tracing the path back to their origins.

The history of gumbo is the story of okra and filé.

2
Okra

Throughout the summer, the Louisiana countryside is full of okra gardens containing an array of cultivars. There are green and red okra pods, fat and skinny varieties, those that look like stars when cut and those that are circular. This year, I'm planting a classic that's green, spineless, and perfectly tender when picked at around three inches—Clemson Spineless, which is an heirloom that was first developed in 1880 by Thomas H. Davis from Lancaster, South Carolina. Davis noticed okra pods without spines in his garden one year. He saved those seeds and planted them the following season, continuing year after year until his entire crop of okra always produced spineless pods. Other heirlooms that do well in Louisiana abound, such as Emerald, Gold Coast, and La Green Velvet, while hybrid options include Green's Best and Cajun Delight.

The beauty of growing okra lies in its simplicity. The plants quickly shoot down long tap roots that keep them alive in even the driest of spells. Eventually, okra reaches up to six feet high with sprawling branches and broad leaves that shade out other plants, reducing the

need for frequent weeding. Pests don't really bother the plants. Neither does disease. The only tender loving care they require is heat and sun—two things we're not lacking in south Louisiana. Even though I'll have to wait two months to get my first pods, my patch of okra will keep producing prolifically until the late fall, when cold fronts usher in frosts.

The old-timers around here caution to not plant okra until around Easter. By then, the threat of freezing temperatures has long passed, the days are consistently warm, and so is the soil, which ensures the seeds have no trouble germinating. This year, though, I'm a little behind. It's late May before I'm in my garden preparing beds—four thirty-foot rows and two fifty-foot. Okra has always fared well here, just a few miles from Arnaudville, even though the soil is comprised of gray clay that's rock solid in dry spells and like, well, gumbo when it rains too much. I sprinkle pelleted chicken manure and compost on the beds before raking it all in. With a garden hoe, I carve out trenches in the soil, placing a seed every six inches or so. After the plants pop up, I'll thin them so they're spaced at least a foot apart. I had soaked my seeds in water the night before—another tip from old-timers—to help promote germination in only two days or so.

I start doing the math in my head. Let's say I get 20 okra pods per plant throughout the season—a modest estimate—and I'll have a plant per foot. That's 220 plants, meaning I'll harvest about 4,000

Opposite: Okra arrived on American shores with enslaved West Africans who had been using the pods in soups for generations. Eventually, these okra soups became today's gumbo. (Photo by Rory Doyle)

pods this season. With this much okra, I'll be able to store away in my freezer a year's supply of okra for gumbo, with plenty left over for friends, family, and neighbors. Truth be told, I haven't always been such a big okra fan. The pods produce a thick, gelatinous substance called mucilage when sliced, and the more you slice them, the more oozes out. Of course, to the unknowing cook, this slime seems an impossible impediment to working with the pods—as it did for me. Yet, after learning how to tame the slime or, in some cases, embrace it, I figured out that okra is one of my favorite summer vegetables.

For those wishing to subdue the sliminess, deep- or pan-frying works well—and this is how many southerners enjoy summer okra. Louisianans haven't ever worried much about mucilage as they have been more concerned about the pods' ability to thicken soups. Okra's slime has long been a perfect way to thicken gumbo in Louisiana, stewed long and slow for hours. And this is how many people cook with the pods. In Brazil's northeastern Bahia state, many Afro-Brazilians make *caruru,* a thick porridge of okra, palm oil, shrimp, onions, and toasted nuts. Brazilians also make *frango com quiabo,* a chicken and okra stew, containing a rich, brown broth that is often served over rice. *Quimbombó guisado* is a Puerto Rican dish that features okra stewed with onions, bell peppers, pork, garlic, tomatoes, and spices to be served over rice. On the islands of Curaçao and Aruba, *giambo* is an okra soup with seafood or beef, also called *yambo.*

These stewed okra dishes were birthed in regions that encompass the West African diaspora—and it's no coincidence that their names and composition look very similar to Louisiana's gumbo. Everywhere that West Africans had a hand in regional cuisine, there is evidence of stewed okra.

* * *

Okra is a member of the mallow family, related to both cotton and hibiscus. It's believed to have first been cultivated in either West Africa or northeastern Africa, near the Nile Valley, thousands of years ago. Writing for *64 Parishes,* Jessica B. Harris noted that okra first appears in the historical record in a letter from 1216 penned by a Spanish traveler who was in Egypt. Eventually, through trade routes, okra ended up in China and India. Harris noted that some speculate the Portuguese could have brought the plant to the Americas in the 1600s. By 1637, okra was established in Brazil, according to Chris Smith in his book *The Whole Okra: A Seed to Stem Celebration.* In the early eighteenth century, okra is recorded as flourishing in Jamaica by the naturalist Sir Hans Sloane, who spent time on the island between 1687 and 1689. By 1748, Peter Kalm, a Finnish-Swedish botanist, wrote of okra in Philadelphia. Even Thomas Jefferson recorded in *Notes on the State of Virginia,* which he began writing in 1781, that okra grew in gardens around the Commonwealth.

Okra likely got from West Africa to the Western Hemisphere on slave ships transporting people on the Middle Passage, a harrowing journey that took the lives of as many of 20 percent of the people aboard before ever reaching the New World due to disease and starvation. Between the sixteenth and nineteenth centuries, up to twenty million people endured the horrors of the six- to ten-week journey across the Atlantic Ocean. Some postulate that Africans braided okra seeds in their hair, thus toting them to North America, where they could grow the plant. Michael W. Twitty, the James Beard Award–winning author of *The Cooking Gene: A Journey through African American Culinary History in the Old South,* a memoir and account of southern cuisine, is skeptical of that account. Instead, he told me that slave traders studied African ethnic groups in order to better exploit them. In particular, by understanding the food of the people they wanted to enslave, slave traders could better manipulate them. So, on Middle Passage ships, the crews transported things like okra seeds so that they could be grown in the New World for enslaved people. Slave traders could then mitigate homesickness and speed up what Twitty called a "seasoning process" of acclimating African people to a lifetime of chattel slavery.

The first enslaved Africans arrived in New Orleans in 1719. The city had only just been established a year earlier. At that time, the region was home to Native Americans like the Atakapa and Chitimacha. But for Europeans, the colony of Louisiana wasn't much more than a backwater outpost rife with disease that was stocked full of soldiers and criminals. France had initiated a forced emigration policy, sending to Louisiana "army deserters, vagabonds, beggars, prostitutes, indigents, and other outcasts," making it a "de facto penal colony," according to Carl Brasseaux in *French, Cajun, Creole, Houma.* Although the deportations eventually ceased, France struggled to attract people to Louisiana for decades. Brasseaux noted that the influx of enslaved Africans during the French period peaked in the early 1720s: "Of the 5,951 [West Africans] known to have been introduced into Louisiana between 1719 and 1763, 5,470 (92 percent) arrived before 1730. Two-thirds of these [enslaved people] were drawn from Senegambia, where the Company of the Indies owned the slave concession." Senegambia refers to a geographic region of West Africa, situated between the Senegal and Gambia Rivers. The peoples who called this region home included those such as the Wolof, Fulbe, and Mandinka. Brasseaux noted, however, that the vast majority of those from Senegambia brought to Louisiana were Bambara, a Mande people from present-day Mali.

By 1741, there were four enslaved Blacks for every 1.2 free whites in the Louisiana colony, according to Gwendolyn Midlo Hall in *Africans in Colonial Louisiana: The Development of Afro-Creole Culture in the Eighteenth Century.* In 1762, Louisiana was ceded to Spain, just before the end of the French and Indian War. Hall noted that the African slave trade in Louisiana during the Spanish period was not well-documented, so it's difficult to know the origins of all of the enslaved people who arrived. However, Hall used inventories of enslaved people from Pointe Coupee Parish in Louisiana to get a better idea. "The Africans brought to Louisiana under Spanish rule came from four main areas: Senegambia, the Bight of Benin, the Bight of Biafra, and Central Africa," she wrote. The Bight of Benin is a bay area in the Gulf of Guinea, once called the Slave Coast, where peoples like the Fon and Mina originated. In the Bight of Biafra, along the Gulf to the southeast, originated peoples such as the Igbo, and then the Kongo came from Central Africa.

Due to the prevalence of Senegambians throughout the French and Spanish colonial period, Hall noted that they were critical to the establishment of Louisiana's Afro-Creole culture, particularly the Bambara people. The Bambara were concentrated in Bambarana, near the upper reaches of the Senegal River and close to the Niger River. Hall noted that agriculture was the Bambara's principal labor, and they often grew grains like millet and sorghum. In the Senegal River Valley, people grew rice and raised cattle and fowl, which was featured prominently in the region's cuisine. Closer to the coast, people often ate seafood. Of course, okra was also being grown in these fertile river valleys that comprise Senegambia. When these skilled agriculturalists arrived in Louisiana, with a climate not all that much different from their own, they continued growing okra to be stewed down in dishes like *soupikandia,* a Senegalese okra soup made with seafood and rice.

Soupikandia and similar okra stews comprised the building blocks of today's soupy gumbo. With these African peoples, we also find gumbo's linguistic origins. Hall noted that, in the Bambara language, which is of the Mande family of languages in West Africa, *gombo* means okra. In many of the Bantu languages of Africa, *gombo* is also a common name for okra: *cigombo* in Lucazi, *kingombo* in Kimbundu, and *ingombo* in Mbuun. For the Fon, okra is *fevi.* According to the *Dictionary of Louisiana French: As Spoken in Cajun, Creole, and American Indian Communities,* both *gombo* and *févi* can refer to okra in Louisiana French, as well as in Louisiana Creole, a creolized language born in Louisiana in the eighteenth century (not to be confused with the Creole identity marker). As is common in Louisiana, when gumbo was made with okra, in French it was called *gombo févi* to distinguish it from *gombo filé,* another version that's thickened with ground sassafras leaves.

By the time the United States bought Louisiana in 1803, the coastal region had undergone the beginning of a mass influx of refugees from the French colony of Saint-Domingue, present-day Haiti. Between 1792 and 1809, at least 11,000 people fled to Louisiana after the beginning of a rebellion in 1791, morphing into the Haitian Revolution, which ended in 1804 with the region's liberation from France. Brasseaux wrote that these French-speaking immigrants were mostly white until 1809; in that year the group included 2,731 whites, 3,102 free persons of color, many of whom were from mixed racial backgrounds, and 3,226 enslaved Blacks. "These French-speaking immigrants, who constituted Louisiana's largest and most racially diverse immigrant group to date, literally doubled the size of the Crescent City's population and preserved New Orleans' French character for two generations."

It's likely that the rapid influx of Haitians to New Orleans contributed to the evolution of gumbo at this time. In a 2022 interview, University of Louisiana at Lafayette (ULL) folklorist John Laudun told the *Advocate,* a Baton Rouge newspaper, that using tomatoes in gumbo likely came from Haitians and was later reinforced by Italian immigration to the city. "Tomatoes in gumbo seem to have the highest density of occurrences in New Orleans, where both a large number of Haitian Creoles settled but also Italians," Laudun said. "As you move away from New Orleans, the density of their usage in gumbo drops off considerably, though pockets along the bayous Teche, Lafourche and

Terrebonne are not unknown." Haitians of African descent had been cooking with tomatoes in the Caribbean long before they arrived in Louisiana. And today, Haitians still prepare a tomato and okra stew with meats called *kalalou,* which some refer to as Haitian gumbo.

The tomato, native to the Andes Mountains of South America, likely was brought to the Caribbean in the sixteenth century, before the establishment of European colonial outposts in North America. Tomatoes appear frequently in early recipes for okra stews and gumbo throughout the African and Haitian diaspora, which ranges from New Orleans and the American South to the East Coast. Often, these recipes are credited to the West Indies. In addition to Mary Randolph's 1824 gumbo recipe, others associated the dish with the West Indies, too, as shown in an 1817 article in a newspaper called the *American Star* from Petersburg, Virginia. Two stewed okra recipes appeared, one that contained tomatoes. The writer noted of the dishes that at St. Domingo, located on the Caribbean island of Hispaniola, "they are called gambo." In an 1831 excerpt in the *New England Farmer,* a recipe for "gombo" that included stewing okra and tomatoes for an hour is described as "a favorite West India dish."

In 1808, the United States officially banned the import of enslaved people to the country. That led New Orleans to become America's largest domestic slave market, where ultimately more than 135,000 people were sold into bondage. The city, a vital port on the Mississippi River, was also a hub for products produced by enslaved people, such as cotton, tobacco, and sugar. After Louisiana achieved statehood in 1812, New Orleans quickly grew to become one of the biggest and most profitable cities in the United States. New Orleans's influence on the rest of America only increased as the nineteenth century progressed. While recipes from Anglo-Americans of the early nineteenth century associate gumbo with the West Indies, after a few decades of New Orleans influence trickling throughout the country, it's evident that perceptions of the dish had changed. Eliza Leslie's *Directions for Cookery,* published in 1840, described a gumbo made with okra, tomatoes, and onions as "a favourite New Orleans dish." *The Carolina Housewife* by Sarah Rutledge, published in 1847, included a recipe for "New Orleans Gumbo." While the dish had long been beloved in New Orleans and Louisiana, by the mid-nineteenth century, among other Americans it had become associated with the Crescent City and its Creoles.

Despite the clear African influence on gumbo, recipes by Black cooks don't appear until after the Civil War. The earliest written accounts of gumbo recipes come from white authors, like Leslie or Rutledge, who were often anglophone women interpreting these dishes from enslaved Blacks or French-speaking Creoles. One of the earliest gumbo recipes that came directly from a Louisiana Creole of color is that of Alexander Dimitry, who published a *gombo filé* recipe in *Le Meschacébé* in 1873. Abby Fisher, a former enslaved person from Mobile, Alabama, wrote the second-known cookbook penned by an African American woman, published in 1881, called *What Mrs. Fisher Knows about Southern Cooking.* Although she was illiterate, Fisher dictated to a writer her recipes that she crafted after thirty-five years "in the art of cooking Soups, Gumbos" and more. She included three gumbo recipes: oyster gumbo soup, made with chicken and thickened with filé; an okra gumbo; and chicken gumbo thickened with okra.

Cookbooks by white authors continued to interpret recipes from Black Creoles, such as *The Creole Cookery Book,* published in 1885. In its preface, the authors wrote that the "occult science" of gumbo should be transmitted from Black Creoles to allow "its proper place in the gastronomical world."

In *The Picayune's Creole Cook Book,* published in New Orleans in 1901, the authors noted a similar mission to preserve old recipes that were in danger of changing due to the disappearance of Black Creole cooks who, after the Civil War, "felt a pride and honor, even in poverty, to cling to the fortunes of their former masters and mistresses." Therefore, the mission of the authors was to preserve these recipes before the "cooks of ante-bellum days have passed away." The authors go on to whitewash Louisiana's culinary history by presenting a Eurocentric claim that Black Creole women "of nearly two hundred years ago, carefully instructed and directed by their white Creole mistresses, who received their inheritance of gastronomic lore from France, where the art of good cooking first had birth, faithfully transmitted their knowledge to their progeny." According to the text, Spanish influences then melded with French culinary tradition to create New Orleans's unique cuisine, leaving out African and Indigenous contributions.

This Eurocentric tale of Louisiana and New Orleans cuisine persisted in cookbooks throughout the twentieth century. Lolis Eric Elie, a New Orleans–born documentarian and author, told me that in his research, he came to understand that these old cookbook introductions were often penned by amateurs who hadn't done any real research. That's why they can often contain historical inaccuracies. "But what makes their approach important and interesting is that there are certain mistakes that they did not make," Elie said. "They didn't fail to credit the French, they seldom failed to credit the Spanish, but they always failed to credit the West Africans." In acknowledging the European influence on New Orleans cuisine, Elie said Black contributions were often explained as a by-product of European direction: "It was crucial to the project of America's racism that the absolute inferiority of the African be established at every turn. In those areas that we were allowed to dominate, it was still crucial to argue that it was white instruction that allowed Black competence to flourish."

Only recently has credit been given to the Black Creoles who shaped Louisiana's culinary landscape. Elie pointed out that one of the most important works that paved the way for this sort of discourse was Nathaniel Burton and Rudy Lombard's 1978 book *Creole Feast: 15 Master Chefs of New Orleans Reveal Their Secrets.* The work is a collection of more than two hundred New Orleans recipes cooked by fifteen Black chefs in the city, including legends like Leah Chase, Austin Leslie, and Louis Evans. In the introduction, Lombard pointed out the "single, lasting characteristic of Creole cuisine is the Black element." Importantly, this work argued what was then a novel idea among the popular culinary discourse, but what had always been true—Black Creoles had long been doing the cooking in New Orleans, leaving an indelible mark on the region's cuisine.

Then came Jessica B. Harris's 1989 *Iron Pots and Wooden Spoons: Africa's Gifts to New World Cooking,* which linked Cajun, Creole, and Caribbean dishes to West and Central Africa. "That is the first book that really addresses this connection in a serious way," Ellie said.

Writers have continued to build upon the body of work representing African contributions to American foodways, such as Twitty's *The Cooking Gene.* While those like JJ Johnson and Alexander Smalls, authors of *Between Harlem and Heaven: Afro-Asian-American Cooking for Big Nights, Weeknights, and Every Day,* have explored the melding of different diasporas and how that has changed the way America eats.

Elie has worked to highlight the African contributions to New Orleans cuisine since the late 1990s, which has involved digging into the origins of gumbo for publications like *Oxford American* and *Smithsonian Magazine.* He went to Senegal in West Africa, one of the places that birthed gumbo. There, he sampled local rice-based dishes that tasted and smelled familiar, ultimately establishing a physical link that he had long written about. "It was like going back home," he told me. "It opened my eyes to seeing the connection of Creole cuisine and African cuisine."

* * *

It's early August, and by now my okra plants tower over my head. I harvest every two days in order to keep up with the prolific growth. I shove aside tired-sized leaves with sprawling branches so that I can enter the garden's shaded walkway. All I can see around me is a jumble of stems, leaves, flowers, and okra pods. Grasshoppers as big as the pods hop away as I approach. Bugs buzz and chirp. Birds swoop overhead, looking for a snack. Like always, I keep a close eye near my feet in case a snake slithers by. Today, like every harvest day, I don pants, a rain jacket with the hood on, and gloves, even though it's nearly 100 degrees and there is no chance of rain. Hairlike spines cover okra plants, and when your skin makes contact with them repeatedly, it can cause itching and redness. Some folks are more sensitive than others, but even just a portion of skin that's exposed to the plants can cause enough discomfort to drive you out of the okra patch.

I make my way down the first row, snapping off okra and tossing them into a five-gallon bucket, listening with a satisfying glee each time a pod clunks on the plastic bottom. The pods are small and finger-long, so they're tender and easily snap off. Though some like their okra to grow six inches long or more, I prefer the smaller ones, which are good for eating fresh in salads, as well as cooked down in a gumbo, pan-fried, or pickled. Wait too long to harvest and the pods get fibrous and hard. By the time I scour the last row, the bucket is half-full. At this rate, I had begun to collect more okra than I can put away. I cut some up and freeze them. Some days I cook a batch fresh; other days I give my entire daily haul to friends and family. But until the first freeze, which is still months away, the okra will keep growing, and my routine will remain.

Today's haul has a specific purpose—it's destined for a soup. I elect to forgo my family's traditional way of cooking okra—in a gumbo—in favor of a recipe I found by Twitty that I had stumbled across on a food blog. In it, Twitty discussed okra's early history in North America from the perspective of Africans. Since okra soup served as the precursor to Louisiana gumbo, I wanted to taste what those early dishes would've been like without sausage, roux, and filé. I figured that I could write about gumbo's history all day long, but to taste its origins would be an experience all on its own.

Twitty based his recipe on nineteenth-century okra dishes from

The Virginia House-wife and *Fifty Years in a Maryland Kitchen.* He combined the heirloom recipes because, as he explained when he and I talked, he thought the mix of elements from both cookbooks better encapsulated an early okra soup. "I wanted them to represent the entire Tidewater [region of the East Coast] and the varieties of ways that food could be responded to," he said. This way, Twitty's rendition is a mix of Maryland and Virginia okra soups, originally cooked by Africans and likely pretty similar to what also existed in Louisiana in the eighteenth century.

When I get home that afternoon, I wash the okra well, then begin slicing them into spheres. I lightly brown onions and bell peppers in butter, toss in some vegetable stock, diced tomatoes, and spices, which stew for a half hour. Then the sliced okra goes in the pot for another half hour. Toward the end, I add garlic and parsley. As I ladle the soup onto a steaming scoop of rice, my mind drifts to the myriad of ways these ingredients first entered the pot. Some from Africa, others from South America. When I take my first bite, the flavors meld perfectly, and I can see why similar dishes were such early favorites in Louisiana.

Today, many African peoples are still stewing okra as their ancestors had. In Gambia, you can find *superkanja,* a stew packed with okra, leafy greens, onions, peppers, and meat or seafood, which is served with rice. To the south in Ghana, there is *banku* and *okro* stew, a tomato-and-okra broth eaten with dumplings. Of course, many more okra soups and stews abound in Africa, where the okra plant is beloved and still grown in abundance.

Without African peoples such as the Wolof, Bambara, Fon, or Mandinka, there would be no gumbo in the Americas at all—not to mention other important culinary favorites and traditions that have shaped American history. "The spirit of Africa is so irreplaceable," Twitty said, "that you can't talk about gumbo without acknowledging it on every single page."

The leaves of the sassafras tree are used to produce filé, an important gumbo ingredient since at least the eighteenth century. Before then, Native Americans used filé to thicken and flavor all sorts of soups. (Photo by Rory Doyle)

3

Sassafras

The sassafras tree has a long and storied past in North America. It's found across Louisiana, extending along the East Coast and interior South and into the southernmost reaches of Canada. Native Americans have used the tree for centuries. The Choctaw, for example, ground the leaves into a powder so that they could sprinkle it in soups, which added flavor and thickened the broth. The sassafras root bark was boiled in order to relieve ailments, such as upset stomach. After Europeans arrived in North America, they began consuming this root bark tea. Of course, root beer was initially flavored with sassafras roots. As early as 1578, Sir Walter Raleigh toted sassafras across the Atlantic to England. Eventually, the plant was heralded as a cure-all that was purported to, among other claims, delay old age or treat syphilis.

The tree's reputation extended beyond medicinal or culinary properties, with some even claiming that Bible boxes made with sassafras wood could ward off evil spirts. In Eric Sloane's 1965 *A Rev-*

erence for Wood, he wrote that it was believed a ship's hull containing enough sassafras wood could provide safety at sea. The tree's root bark was used to scent perfume and soaps. Due to the European obsession with the tree, in the seventeenth century sassafras was, alongside tobacco, one of the biggest exports from North America.

In the twentieth century, scientists discovered that a compound found in sassafras roots, called safrole, caused cancer in lab rats over an extended period of time. By this point, sassafras's popularity had declined anyway, but the research led to a ban of safrole by the Food and Drug Administration. The European Commission lists safrole as carcinogenic. Although foods we eat often, like nutmeg, contain safrole, the substance is found in high concentrations in sassafras roots. The substance contains methylenedioxyamphetamine, or MDA, which is a hallucinogen deemed a Schedule 1 controlled substance by the US Drug Enforcement Agency. Root beer consumed today typically includes safrole-free sassafras or artificial flavors. However, the leaves contain negligible levels of safrole and have been cleared by the FDA, which is why it's legal to use them today as a spice.

Since the eighteenth century, Louisiana Creoles have added ground sassafras leaves, called filé by the French, to their gumbos in a continuation of Choctaw tradition. Even today, filé is a popular ingredient in Louisiana gumbo, available commercially from brands like Zatarain's and Tony Chachere's. Historically, though, sassafras

Opposite: Dusty Fuqua learned the art of harvesting sassafras and making filé from his mentor, John Oswald Colson. Each spring Fuqua collects and processes the leaves to make filé and also works to introduce others to the tradition. (Photo by Rory Doyle)

leaves were plucked fresh from the tree, air-dried, and then ground for use all year. But, today, there aren't many local foragers left.

This cultural loss has beckoned Dusty Fuqua, an anthropologist, to forage for sassafras in Kisatchie National Forest, located near Alexandria, Louisiana. Over the course of a decade, Fuqua learned how to prepare filé from his late mentor John Oswald Colson, who was from central Louisiana's Cane River community. Together, the pair foraged deep in the Kisatchie hills to collect sassafras leaves, which they then processed and bottled to give away to friends and family or to sell at local folklife festivals. Colson, who had African, Indigenous, and European ancestry, served as a link to a storied tradition that rests with the people of the Cane River region. These folks were known to have produced quality filé that was then distributed to the surrounding areas. "Isle Brevelle," an 1897 article from the *Louisiana Populist,* published in Natchitoches, described the customs of the Creoles from Cane River's Isle Brevelle community: "At a dance will be seen a big fire in the yard, and a big pot of gumbo on it . . . This gumbo is made from boiling fresh meat or game with the pulverized leaves and stems of a dwarf sassafras, which grows on the hills, and whither these people go in great numbers at the proper season to gather it."

As far as anyone can tell, Fuqua is among only a few tradition bearers left who still harvest sassafras leaves in the hills near Cane River to make filé the old-fashioned way—foraging and processing mostly by hand. During the height of the COVID-19 pandemic in 2020 and 2021, Fuqua took over Colson's leading role in the harvest and production of filé, a task he has continued since his mentor's passing. Since the folk festivals were shut down at the time, he took to the internet in order to connect to people, in turn selling hundreds of bottles across the United States—with one customer as far away as Germany.

I first met Fuqua in May 2021 at his home in Pineville while I was working on an article for the *Bitter Southerner.* I wanted to dig into the history of the sassafras tree and to better understand how it got so intertwined with gumbo. I had heard about Fuqua and his filé from Instagram, where he was posting foraging pictures and bottles of vibrant, green filé like I had never seen before. I had asked to tag along on one of his outings. He had gladly obliged, only requesting that I come prepared to pick, too. Dusty and I harvested two full crawfish sacks of fresh leaves that morning. Later that afternoon, he showed me how he stores, dries, and processes the leaves in order to get a quality, final product.

Now, it's a year later in June, and I meet back up with Fuqua to pick again. This time, I'm intent on not only foraging but making my own batch of filé. Fuqua, who hadn't yet scored a sizeable load of sassafras, is looking to ramp up his production for the summer. "At the end of the day, it doesn't matter if we sell any bottles or we give it all away," he tells me as we ride north toward Kisatchie. "It's about enhancing the awareness of this tradition." Fuqua is the chief of resource management at Cane River Creole National Historical Park. His expertise is in Louisiana cultural anthropology, which involves early Indigenous cultures. He explains that most of the national forest we'll be walking around today was at one time home to Native American tribes like the Caddo and Atakapa; then eventually the Choctaw arrived in the eighteenth century after being displaced by white Americans in the Southeast. Virtually the entire area was clear-cut, but the federal government purchased the land in the 1930s and returned it to forest. The Kisatchie forest is now comprised of more than 600,000 acres of woodland dotted across parts of central and north Louisiana. Unlike the flat delta terrain to the south, this upland environment encompasses rolling hills, boggy hollows, and cascading waterfalls. These woods are a hotbed of biodiversity, with even minute changes in sunlight availability or soil structure nurturing rare flora like the carnivorous pitcher plant. The forest's prized longleaf pine, brought back to life after near elimination at the hands of loggers, towers atop sandstone bluffs. The pines grow far apart, allowing a dense canopy of smaller trees and shrubs underneath to thrive, such as the sassafras.

Even though it's June, the temperature hovers around a pleasant 80 degrees by the time we get to Kisatchie. Both of us scan the side of the road for any significant patches of sassafras worthy of picking. We stroll at a leisurely pace along a gravel road, so I'm able to spot blooming coral bean bushes, their pink flowers stretching toward the sky, and clasping coneflowers growing in patches wherever the sun's rays could reach through the canopy. Controlled burns have left other parts of the landscape charred and unfit for foraging, but Fuqua explains that the plant life will bounce back quickly. These periodic fires that are set by the Forest Service work to mimic the natural blazes that once were commonplace here.

Eventually, we stumble upon a spot that's rife with the trees. Within a few minutes, we're both stuffing our sacks with handfuls of sassafras—the mature specimens are dark emerald whereas the younger, smaller ones are much paler. The leaves appear in three different forms: oval, trilobate, or mitten-shaped. They're thick and velvety to the touch, staining my fingers green over the course of the morning and covering them with a sweet aroma. To me, it smells like Fruit Loops cereal. "That's what everyone thinks," Fuqua tells me.

Fuqua embodies a quiet focus most of the morning, just as he had the last time we foraged together. It's clear that he holds a deep reverence for this tradition. He tells me that Kisatchie's sassafras trees have become for him a sort of cultural link to the Indigenous people who have shaped our present. "In my opinion it's the best example of a tradition that we learned directly from the Native Americans and we're still doing it now," he explains, referring to transmission of information from Native Americans to Louisiana Creoles. "It's like a link to the past. The people here long before us, thousands of years before us, were using that same tree and its properties. Their gumbo didn't look like ours, but it was something close. It was important to them."

* * *

Traditional Choctaw soups were seasonal and often contained abundant plant material that was either foraged or grown. In *A Culinary History of Pittsburg County: Little Italy, Choctaw Beer and Lamb Fries,* David Cathey mentioned some of them, such as *koshiba,* a soup made with poke leaves that is boiled several times with the option to add fatty meat—the same process applies for stinging nettles and dock. There's also *tanchi labonna,* which involves cooking hominy in a broth, then adding meat, which was likely venison or bear. Cathey wrote that the first-recorded Choctaw recipe, *tanchi okchi* or *sagamité,* dates back to 1755. The Choctaw would grind dried corn kernels and boil them along with beans or pumpkin. Their soups also contained ground sassafras leaves and redbay leaves—two common ingredients in gumbo.

In the mid-eighteenth century, the Choctaw in the Southeast numbered around 20,000, with most of them concentrated in present-day Mississippi. In the colonial period, the state was a part of France's Louisiana colony, which broadly encompassed the Mississippi River Valley. The first capital of the French colony of Louisiana was founded in 1699 and called Fort Maurepas, located in the Biloxi Bay of Mississippi. The French established a close relationship with the Choctaw as English colonists began encroaching from the Atlantic Coast with their Chickasaw allies. The Choctaw and Chickasaw were already engaged in disputes, and they clashed frequently. The French traded with the Choctaw, providing them with clothing and weapons. In turn, the Choctaw promised to help defend against the English and Chickasaw, while providing much-needed rations to French colonists. In an article in *The Mississippi Encyclopedia,* Davis S. Newhall wrote that "the colonists, facing starvation during the first two decades, needed Indian-produced food." Gwendolyn Midlo Hall noted in *Africans in Colonial Louisiana* that Native Americans taught Europeans about the local plants and animals and that at many of the early settlements in Louisiana, the "colonists were socialized to Indian ways of dress, housing, cultivation, and preparation of food."

Opposite: After sassafras is picked, it's air-dried for a month, ground up, and sifted to produce a fine powder. (Photo by Rory Doyle)

It seems inevitable that the French encountered ground sassafras powder and Choctaw soups during this swapping of food in the early 1700s. They took to calling this powder filé, which means *thread* due to the leaves' ability to thicken broths to the point of stringiness. Yet the Choctaw called ground sassafras *kombo ashish,* which has led some to speculate that this word served as the linguistic origin of the modern word *gumbo.* Louisiana historian Shane K. Bernard told me that all the source material that he has seen links the word *gumbo* to West Africa. He explained that he has never seen a historical reference to a pot of gumbo as "kombo." However, in an 1875 article from the *New Orleans Bulletin,* a journalist discussing the Choctaw of northern Lake Pontchartrain wrote that sassafras powder was called "gombo." In *What Mrs. Fisher Knows about Old Southern Cooking,* published in 1881, African American author Abby Fisher's oyster gumbo recipe recommends "stir[ring] into soup one tablespoonful of gumbo quickly" just before serving the dish. This is, of course, referring to ground sassafras. It's unclear why these two sources refer to the powder in this way, but it appears that ground sassafras, at one time, went by names other than just filé. Louisiana francophones might refer to the sassafras tree as *bois de gombo* or gumbo tree. Even today, some members of the United Houma Nation in Louisiana who are from Terrebonne or Lafourche Parish use the words *filé* and *gumbo* interchangeably to refer to powdered sassafras. The Houma language of the United Houma Nation, although much of it is lost to time, is Western Muskogean, which is in the same linguistic family as the Choctaw language. It's possible that, at one time, *kombo ashish* was part of their lexicon as well.

Due to this murky linguistic lineage, Bernard admitted that he can't completely rule out linguistic origins that also lie with the Choctaws' *kombo,* noting that "it's possible [the word *gumbo*] draws on both Choctaw and West African sources."

Danny Petrella, who is a member of the Mamou Choctaw tribe In central Louisiana, believes exactly that. According to oral histories from his ancestors, he told me, okra gumbo and what he called Choctaw gumbo are two distinct dishes with separate origins. Just as the evolution of okra stew included additions from other ethnic groups, Petrella claimed that Choctaw gumbo began with plant material, seafood or other meat, and filé, but then later came the sausage, rice, and cayenne. "The okra gumbo came by the African people," he explained. "That dish kind of intermingled with the Choctaw gumbo and formed a cultural gumbo." Due to physical and linguistic resemblances, Petrella said, the two soups were lumped together as gumbo.

For other groups of Louisiana Native Americans, like the Pointe-au-Chien Indian Tribe and the United Houma Nation, sassafras has also been an important part of their culture as medicine and for use as filé. Janie Verret Luster, a member of the United Houma Nation from Bayou Dularge, told me oral histories suggest that a sort of gumbo thickened with filé has been cooked by the Houma since before the colonial era—back when the Houma were cooking, not out of iron pots, but sacks made with animal skins. Her late mother, Mary Verret, grew a patch of sassafras trees in their yard in order to have a steady supply of filé, as did many neighbors in the community. Typically, she harvested the leaves in August before they turned orange in the fall. Luster recalled, "People would come from near and far to get fresh filé from her."

On his journey on the Mississippi River, the Frenchman René-Robert Cavelier, sieur de La Salle, caught wind in 1682 that the Houma were living on the eastern banks of the river in what is today West Feliciana Parish. The tribe officially made contact with Europeans in 1686 after Henri de Tonti visited their village. Writing for *64 Parishes,* Elizabeth Ellis noted that the tribe was recorded as having 350 men in 1699. "Extremely important to the survival of the early Louisiana colonists, small Native nations supplied French settlers with food and material goods during shortages," Ellis wrote. "Throughout the French colonial period, the Houmas also regularly acted as scouts and supported the French during military conflicts with other American Indian nations."

The Houma continued moving around throughout the eighteenth century. They went south along the Mississippi north of Lake Pontchartrain, and some ventured into Ascension Parish. Eventually, many Houma settled in the vast marshes of Terrebonne and Lafourche Parishes on the coast of Louisiana. After generations of interaction with the French, many Houma have French last names like Dardar and Billiot, and much of the Houma Nation is francophone. But Luster noted that for many Houma, a traditional gumbo doesn't involve the French-inspired roux at all. In fact, a broth thickened with roux is considered by many Houma to be a *fricassée* or a stew. "To me, we have two kinds of gumbo," Luster said; "one is the filé made strictly with filé, and the other is with okra."

The idea, then, is that there were two dishes in early colonial Louisiana: a Native American soup with filé, cooked by peoples such as the Choctaw and the Houma, and also an okra dish stewed up by Africans. Eventually, both of these soups became referred to as gumbo.

There have historically been clear distinctions between gumbo variations based on the substance used to thicken the broth—*gombo févi,* thickened with okra, and *gombo filé,* thickened with ground sassafras. Although today these monikers are far less common, and people tend to amalgamate all versions of gumbo as variations of one dish, since the beginning of gumbo's history these two base ingredients demanded distinct names. In an excerpt Shane K. Bernard drew from P. de la Coudrenière's 1773 account in "Observations sur le sassafras, arbre de l'Amérique," Coudrenière described filé in early Louisiana cuisine: "These leaves used in sauces . . . give them a pleasant taste . . . The gummy principal is so sticky that a pinch of this powder is enough to make a viscous broth. This dish is known as American gombo. But we must distinguish this American stew from the one called gombo févi" [Bernard's translation from French].

Coudrenière's insistence on calling *gombo filé* an American stew might stem from its origins in the New World, though perhaps he was acknowledging that *gombo févi* was, as was well-known at the time, a dish with origins in Africa and the Caribbean. Either way, this distinction displays the importance that once existed in separating these two versions. This early division between types of gumbo morphed into doctrine. Many gumbo recipes from the nineteenth century note this important distinction, as in the following direction from a recipe in Lafcadio Hearn's *La Cuisine Creole:* "Add okra or a preparation of dried and pounded sassafras leaves, called filee. This makes the difference in gombo . . . Either gives the smoothness so desirable in this soup." It was often said that, in line with tradition, one should never add okra and filé in the same pot.

In the nineteenth century, filé was an inseparable part of gumbo. According to some accounts, the powder was the deciding factor that transformed a broth into gumbo. In Alexander Dimitry's 1873 gumbo recipe in *Le Meschacébé,* his broth that had been simmering for hours was rendered gumbo only after his addition of the powder at the end of the process: "Thus far, we have a rich composite stew, which is now to be converted into gombo . . . by sprinkling the sassafras over the liquid, rapidly beating it at the same time with a spoon, thoroughly incorporate the powder with the stock, and . . . the gombo is done."

It's often been said that filé couldn't have developed as an initial, important ingredient in gumbo. The explanation goes that okra, the main gumbo ingredient, was used in the summer while in season, and filé was used to thicken the soups in winter as a sort of substitute. However, okra can be air-dried in Louisiana, especially in the fall months, when humidity is lower and okra plants are still prolifically producing pods. In an 1845 article from the *St. Landry Whig,* published in Opelousas, Louisiana, a journalist wrote of the beauty of growing okra, noting that it "can be dried, and kept good all winter" in the parish. Clearly, folks were drying okra in those days, and it's a good bet they put that dried okra in winter gumbos when a hot broth was well warranted. Hearn featured okra in his recipe called "Maigre Shrimp Gombo for Lent." However, Lent often begins in February, and local okra harvesting isn't in full swing in Louisiana until the summer. This meant that, before refrigeration, people who made Lenten *gombo févi* must have had a supply that was preserved in some way.

Chris Smith, in *The Whole Okra,* tackled the filé origins theory in his book. While he noted filé could have been a seasonal substitute, he also wrote that sassafras could have been used to develop "an individual stew that later melded with the okra preparation and assumed the same name." Others aren't convinced. Cynthia LeJeune Nobles argued in *New Orleans Cuisine* that Choctaw origins of gumbo are unlikely. She noted that gumbo's "historic pairing with rice is one of two convincing reasons why neither Native Americans' stews nor French bouillabaisse morphed into today's soupy gumbo. Native American stews were centered around corn, an ingredient rarely found in gumbo." Although modern gumbos don't contain corn, Coudrenière's eighteenth-century account, which mentions a collection of early gumbo ingredients, challenges Nobles's assertion by displaying that corn was indeed present. Hearn's collection of recipes, published around eighty-five years later, also mentioned adding "green corn" to gumbo, referring to tender sweet corn.

In an essay in *Acadians and Cajuns,* the folklorist John Laudun wrote that rice has reigned supreme as the starch of choice in gumbo bowls only since the late nineteenth century. "Before that, Louisiana cleft more closely to the rest of the South and the starch that gumbo covered was corn meal mush, known at first by the Native American term *sagamité* and later by the African-influenced *couche couche,*" he wrote, adding that the "corn mush consumed by the colonial French and later by the Cajuns was in fact a Native American inheritance . . .

Early gumbos were served over this corn mush." In the writings of a Frenchman named C. C. Robin, who between 1803 and 1805 traveled to Louisiana, there is a description of Acadians eating gumbo over a cornmeal mush. Today, corn has faded into gumbo obscurity as commercial rice agriculture became more common and the dish, which evolved regularly in its infancy, changed as other ingredients became more widely available.

It's not just filé that has Indigenous origins in gumbo. There are many others that came to the gumbo pot by way of Native Americans. The bay leaf, for example, is a staple in gumbo that delivers an aromatic finish. Today, most bay leaves consumed in the United States are culinary bay leaves (*Laurus nobilis*), a plant native to the Mediterranean region. Although, historically, Creoles employed the redbay leaf (*Persea borbonia*), which has a home range in the Southeast. Native Americans had culinary uses for the redbay, but it was better known as a medicine. According to Kim Coder, a forestry professor at the University of Georgia, in an essay about the tree, the Seminole and Creek nations used redbay to treat cough, fever and chills, headaches, kidney problems, and a host of other issues. Typically, the leaves and roots were steeped in teas.

Spicy smoked pork, called tasso, is a popular contemporary gumbo ingredient with Indigenous roots. In a 2016 article in the *Houma Courier,* columnist Bill Ellzey explored tasso's origins, noting that the word is derived from the Spanish *tasajo,* which refers to a slice of cured beef that's been dried. In his column, Ellzey referenced a 1938 newspaper article in the *Lafourche Comet* that points to the

Indigenous origins of tasso, particularly regarding the Houma people of Louisiana's southeastern coast and their dried, smoked fish. This fish tasso was, at one time, a regular ingredient in gumbo for coastal communities. According to the excerpt, folks would gather in the marshes to catch fish. Then they'd smoke the fish filets, sharing with each other while the catch was good. These smoked slabs would last far longer than fresh fish, allowing communities to create food stability in lean times. Tasso would have also encompassed other types of smoked meat, such as venison or bison. Europeans then used this meat curing method and applied it to pork, birthing the modern conception of tasso. In an 1897 edition of the *La Sentinelle de Thibodaux,* a newspaper from Thibodaux, Louisiana, a recipe for *gombo file* recommended first adding tasso to the pot, and then lard and flour for a roux. The excerpt notes in Louisiana Creole: "*yé prend la vianne la qui yé pélé 'tasso,' metté li dans to chodière*" (Put some meat, called "tasso," in your pot).

Often, modern tasso is seasoned with cayenne, and gumbo usually requires a hefty pinch of the seasoning. Cayenne is native to Central and South America, and the plant had been cultivated for thousands of years by Indigenous people. The peppers were brought to Europe by Christopher Columbus in the fifteenth century. Tabasco hot sauce wouldn't be possible without tabasco peppers, which are native to Mexico. Bell peppers, another important gumbo ingredient, were also first cultivated in Central and South America.

While the evidence is clear that gumbo was birthed by West African okra stews, there's ample enough proof that Indigenous soups made a strong mark in the evolution of the dish in Louisiana. Gumbo's evolution is intertwined with the history of Louisiana's Indigenous peoples. Without them, gumbo as we know it wouldn't be possible.

* * *

Deep in the Kisatchie hills, Fuqua and I pick a few leaves from each plant and take care to leave enough on the tree so that it's not bare. He has told me of poachers cutting entire trees and has also witnessed overharvesting where he works in Cane River. While the trees were at one time abundant there, Fuqua says that these days it's hard to even come by a sapling. That's had an impact on the availability of locally sourced filé, too, which used to be commonplace in the Cane River Valley.

Fuqua and I are surrounded by so much sassafras, it's hard for me to imagine a shortage of the trees anywhere. From where I'm standing, sassafras from my knees to above my head extends as far as I can see. At times it's even difficult to spot Fuqua, who has been never more than a dozen yards away. In early June, the leaves are vibrant and fresh, having just grown after winter. Fuqua tells me that Creoles would historically pick the leaves on August 15, the Feast of the Assumption in Catholic tradition. Others would harvest even later in the year, such as in the fall, when the leaves turn brilliant hues of orange and red. While Fuqua has harvested sassafras later in the year, he said it's become harder for him to find quality leaves in late summer and the fall due to insect damage. The yellow poplar weevil is among the culprits. The insect overwinters in leaf litter and emerges in the spring to feed on sassafras leaves. As climate change ushers in warmer weather, the weevils can wreak havoc longer and earlier than they have before.

Sassafras trees are also susceptible to the laurel wilt pathogen, a fungus that was first detected in the United States around 2003—there have been reports of local cases in Kisatchie as early as 2016. The ambrosia beetle, an invasive insect from Asia, can infect swaths of forests in no time. After a sassafras is infected, it can die within weeks. Forest managers currently don't have a viable treatment to slow down the disease's spread. Laurel wilt also affects redbay and avocado trees, which for the latter is a threat to agricultural operations in California and Central and South America.

Environmental factors cloud the future of the waning local filé production, but Fuqua acknowledges that loss of tradition has been the most salient factor in the decline. Younger folks aren't picking up the ways of the old-timers. Fuqua estimates that many people are just oblivious to the fact that filé, even though it's well-known among Louisianans, is actually ground sassafras leaves from trees that grow abundantly all across the state. The traditional ways of processing sassafras leaves by hand are slipping away, too.

There are some accounts that display how sassafras was processed in Louisiana. Coudrenière's 1784 work noted that sassafras is harvested in July, dried in the open air, and then pulverized. Between 1908 and 1909, the ethnographer David I. Bushnell Jr. visited a community of Choctaw near Bayou Lacombe in Louisiana, located on the northern shore of Lake Pontchartrain north of New Orleans. He compiled a report for the Smithsonian Institution titled *The Choctaw of Bayou Lacomb, St. Tammany Parish, Louisiana.* His notes included incredible details about these people, such as their myths and legends, ornaments, pastimes, and music. Bushnell recorded little information regarding traditional foodways, but he was able to collect material on seven traditional plants, sassafras being one of them, which he labeled as "kombo ashish."

> The leaves of Laurus sassafras are gathered during the autumn, usually about the middle of October, after they have turned red. They are thoroughly dried in the sun and air, without the use of artificial heat. They are then pounded in a wooden mortar until reduced to a very fine powder, which is sifted to remove all hard particles. The powder is again placed in the mortar and pounded until as fine as it can be made, when it is ready for use. About a teaspoonful of this powder added to a kettle of soup gives it a glutinous quality and the flavor also is relished. This powder is highly prized by the Creoles of Louisiana.

The mortar and pestle were traditionally made out of wood. The mortar is called a *pilé* in French, and the pestle is *pilon.* Fuqua uses a mortar and pestle in demonstrations at the Cane River National Historical Park. When he's processing sassafras on his own, although he employs a mechanical blender, everything is done by hand. While I won't be using a mortar and pestle, I want to stick to tradition as much as possible. When I get home from our Kisatchie forage, I dump my sack full of freshly picked leaves on my kitchen table and spread them out as evenly as possible so they could air-dry. I leave them there for a month, and every few days I flip them so they all dry at an even rate—upon counsel from Fuqua, I use a stick so that the oil from my hands doesn't damage the leaves.

When processing day comes, I gather all the tools necessary: a sifter, a glass bowl, and a blender. I begin by removing the petiole and midrib of each leaf to be discarded. I crush the blade and toss it into the blender. After blending I sift the powder, which removes any leftover chunks or veins of the leaves. The end result is a vivid-green powder with sharp, aromatic nodes. Although commercial filé is available at most Louisiana grocery stores, the difference between store-bought filé and this homemade variety is stark. Fuqua has called store-bought filé "sawdust," a brown powder that is a by-product due to, as he estimates, grinding up stems and branches instead of carefully sifting it all, and then from the powder sitting on store shelves for months. After having tasted both versions, I vow to never eat commercial filé ever again—it's simply tasteless compared to the fresh kind.

While not everyone will be willing to forage the woods for sassafras, Fuqua believes that the quality of his product—aromatic and packing a tasteful punch—will entice others to seek out locally sourced, traditionally made filé. He invites along on his picks anyone who is willing to learn and sweat a little bit. He started the Sassafras Society a few years ago, comprised of a group of friends interested in making filé. One day, he hopes to turn the group into a nonprofit in order to educate a new generation about sassafras and filé.

I bottle dozens of one-ounce glass containers of filé, which I will give away to anyone who might be interested in what fresh filé tastes like in gumbo. The flavor, I'll tell them, just can't be replicated—a sharp snap of floral nodes that perfectly complements a rich, roux broth. Like Fuqua, I have hopes that these folks might pass on the word about the superior quality of fresh, locally harvested filé. In this way, traditions are being passed on so that a piece of gumbo history won't be forgotten.

4

Creole or Cajun?

As I navigate the aisles at a neighborhood grocery store, my eyes scan the myriad of local food items you'll be hard-pressed to find anywhere but south Louisiana. I'm not talking farm-to-table staples, but hyper-local regional foodstuffs with strange-sounding names that'll make most anglophones' tongues twist. In the frozen food aisle, there is Savoie's boudin and andouille, and I snag the latter for an upcoming gumbo. Adjacent to the rice I pass Zatarain's Jambalaya Mix and Tony Chachere's Creole Etouffee Base Mix. Our locally produced Steen's cane syrup is better stocked than the nearby Log Cabin and Hungry Jack.

I make it to the spice aisle to re-up my supply of a favorite blend, Slap Ya Mama Cajun Seasoning, made with salt, red pepper, black pepper, and garlic. Out of curiosity, I pick up an adjacent can of Tony's Chachere's Original Creole Seasoning, a blend of salt, red pepper, black pepper, chili powder, and dehydrated garlic. Each company was founded only a few miles apart, one in Opelousas and the other just

Seasoning blends abound in Louisiana, purporting to be Cajun or Creole, even though the majority of them look more or less the same. The discrepancy comes down to complex identity markers in Louisiana that have shaped how people view themselves and their food. (Photo by author)

down the road in Ville Platte. But here are two distinct monikers—Cajun and Creole—to describe a nearly identical mix of seasonings.

I keep scanning the spice options, and the varied labels continue. Zatarain's Creole Seasoning. Louisiana Cajun Seasoning. Konriko Creole Seasoning. And perhaps the most confusing of them all, Cajun's Choice Creole Seasoning made by Acadian Kitchens. Each one of these blends looks, more or less, the same.

Interested in the andouille's branding made by Savoie's that I have in my cart, I pick it up and begin reading. On the front label, I see that this product is "Produced the Cajun way." In the top left corner, a round label reads "Certified Cajun." Elsewhere on the package, I spot "Real Cajun." I'd been informed of this product's Cajun-ness three times already and figure it wasn't by mistake. I look again at the can of Slap Ya Mama, and it also contains the "Certified Cajun" label. The word *Cajun* appears five more times on the can.

Turns out, the "Certified Cajun" label is doled out by the Louisiana Department of Agriculture and Forestry, part of a state program designed to inform people that a product is mostly of Louisiana origin. The department also offers "Certified Creole" as an option for local businesses to use on their products. In order to qualify for the label of Cajun, a product "must be representative of the culture that is generally of Acadian descent." While in order to use the "Certified Creole" label, a product "shall be of Creole heritage." Without any further definition on the department's website, these distinctions seem a little ambiguous. After all, what in Louisiana is of Acadian descent and what is Creole?

The question lingers with me on the drive home when I notice a billboard hugging Interstate 49 that is advertising Prejean's restaurant. The billboard reads "Prejean's . . . simply Cajun." The Prejean's menu boasts familiar items like gumbo but also ethnic fusions like crawfish enchiladas, crawfish rolls, boudin flatbread, and quesadillas. It seems like if a Cajun cooks a taco, it's now a Cajun taco.

In reality, there isn't much about Cajun that is simple. The word is a corruption of "Acadian," which describes a francophone ethnic group that sailed from France to the Maritime provinces of Eastern Canada in the 1600s and who were eventually exiled by the British—a sizeable group of them sought refuge in south Louisiana. While the Acadians have been important to the region's culture and history, the Cajun label has come to disproportionately represent much of south Louisiana's unique character after having been commodified, packaged, and marketed into a brand. As Barry Ancelet, a retired folklorist at the University of Louisiana at Lafayette (ULL), once quipped, "One can now fish out of a Cajun brand bass boat with Cajun brand bait, and put the catch in a Cajun brand ice chest filled with Cajun brand ice."

The Cajun branding craze has impacted how Louisianans discuss the history of the region's cuisine, which has therefore informed how America and the rest of the world views Louisiana cooking. To better understand how Cajun and, thus, Acadian has come to reign supreme in Louisiana, it's best to start with a much earlier term—Creole.

* * *

The ethnomusicologist Alan Lomax, who in the 1930s with his father, John, recorded traditional Louisiana music for the Library of Congress, was instrumental in helping preserve early Cajun and zydeco music. These treasured recordings are still being studied today. After having spent ample time over the years with the people of south Louisiana, In 1991 Alan made a documentary called *Cajun Country* where he captured the rich musical flair of the region. He described the area itself as Cajun Country, which in the documentary, he surmised "was settled by French speakers from Canada, and they absorbed and Cajunized their local Indian neighbors and the settlers who came later on from various parts of Europe and from Africa and the West Indies. Out of this mix came a new culture, with its own cuisine, and its own music."

Alan's watered-down, Cajun-centric version of south Louisiana's history makes a useful soundbite, but in reality, it doesn't tell the whole story at all—and it's only remotely accurate. But it's a narrative that has been repeated for several decades, perpetuated by academics, writers, tourism departments, and Louisianans themselves. This has been problematic. As Carl Brasseaux wrote in *French, Cajun, Creole, Houma,* scholarship that has disproportionately focused on Cajuns has "tended to mask the great cultural, racial, and ethnic diversity in Louisiana's French-speaking region, an area that ethnographers have come to regard in recent years as the home of North America's most complex rural society."

The Creole label, also common in Louisiana, is much older than Cajun. According to Brasseaux, the word Creole means native or indigenous to a specific area, and the term has continually evolved over the years. The French word *créole* is derived from the Spanish word *criollo,* which was used in Spanish New World settlements to denote enslaved people as early as the 1560s. However, the term evolved to include native-born whites in South America—those with Spanish or European roots who were born in the Americas. Brasseaux noted that in many islands of the West Indies, including the French colony of Saint-Domingue, Creole applied to native-born people of all racial groups. "This usage was transplanted to Louisiana," he wrote, continuing, "In early Louisiana the term meant the descendants of pioneers—French, Spanish, German, Irish, Italian, sometimes even English, and African—who were born in the region prior to the Louisiana Purchase." According to Cécyle Trépanier, in her work "The Cajunization of French Louisiana," after the Louisiana Purchase in 1803, "the Creoles added to the definition a cultural dimension to exclude the American newcomers. To be Creole one needed to be native and French in culture."

As more Anglo-Americans began encroaching on Louisiana's heavily francophone region, they did not fully grasp the state's mixture of ethnicity that was not based on the same bifurcated racial rules as the rest of the American South. In Louisiana, there existed a complex society that was comprised of many different francophone or creolophone ethnic groups like white planters, Black planters, whites or free people of color who were tradesmen or craftsmen, people of mixed-race ancestry, poor whites who practiced subsistence farming, and enslaved Blacks. The term Creole could, essentially, refer to any of them.

The end of the Civil War and the era of Jim Crow greatly impacted the dynamic of Louisiana's cultural landscape. By then, the notion of racial purity had consumed the South, and many whites, especially anglophones, were skeptical of Louisiana's Creole moniker, which was based on culture, language, and "nativeness" rather than skin color. Trépanier noted that ruptures in identity markers began occurring. There were labels like white Creoles and Black Creoles, and at times the Creole label denoted higher socioeconomic status. Eventually, whites began dropping the Creole label altogether, embracing English and conforming to southern Anglo values that demanded adherence to a white-black duality. Any Creoles who could pass as white did so to escape the prejudices of Jim Crow, leaving more Black Louisianans who retained the Creole label.

Around four decades before the Louisiana Purchase, in 1764, French-speaking Acadians from Canada began arriving in Louisiana after being exiled by the British. Originally from western France, they had established prosperous outposts mostly in Nova Scotia in the 1600s, forming a tight-knight ethnic community. By 1785, about three thousand of these exiles had sought refuge in south Louisiana, which was then a Spanish colony that was still heavily francophone and Catholic. Many of them first settled along the Mississippi River near the German Coast, and then along Bayous Teche and Lafourche. In an essay titled "How Much Acadian Is There in Cajun?" Thomas Klingler, a French professor at Tulane University, noted that by the time the last group of Acadians arrived, there were already more than forty-two thousand Creoles in the Louisiana colony: "The Acadians, then, arrived as a minority in a colony with well-established French-speaking populations that had originally come from France, Quebec, and, in the case of French-speaking [enslaved people], Africa. Moreover, in the ensuing years, the number of Acadian immigrants was dwarfed by that of new francophone groups arriving from France and from the former French colony of St. Domingue, following the slave revolt there that resulted in the founding of the republic of Haiti." The influx of Haitians to Louisiana, whether white or Black, was also regarded as Creole as the term was already well-established in the Caribbean. Klingler pointed out that, although the newly arrived Acadians were influential due to their cohesiveness and numerous offspring, this small group did not subsume the larger French-speaking Creole population. Rather, it was the other way around, as the group was assimilated into the larger Creole culture of south Louisiana—especially when Acadians were the minority in a particular community. Meaning that, among other cultural practices, the Acadians adopted new ways of cultivating crops and cooking dishes like gumbo, made with local ingredients they were initially unfamiliar with such as cayenne peppers, okra, or filé.

Acadian morphed into Cajun rather gradually, and the transformation is just as complex as that of Creole identity. According to Jacques Henry in "From 'Acadien' to 'Cajun' to 'Cadien': Ethnic Labelization and Construction of Identity," throughout most of the nineteenth century the Acadian identity marker was the most common way to describe the ethnic group. Acadian was also associated with labels such as French, but people also considered the Acadians to be Creoles. There is evidence of the abbreviated Cajun label as early as 1851, nearly one hundred years after the arrival of the first Acadians in Louisiana. In *Le Pionnier de l'Assomption,* a francophone newspaper from Napoleonville, Louisiana, the word *cadien* appears, which is the French spelling of Cajun. However, as Henry noted, Acadian and

Cajun/*cadien* weren't synonymous. He wrote that after the Civil War, the diverse Acadian socioeconomic group of tradesmen, farmers, and professionals was divided into two: an upper-class Acadian group influenced by Anglo-American culture, and the most populous segment, consisting of impoverished, poorly educated people who were dubbed Cajuns. The differences between Acadians and Cajuns were those of social class, while Creole became increasingly aligned with Blacks who spoke either French or Louisiana Creole. Henry wrote that Cajun was a "corrupted term to be used with precaution because it is an insult." For example, in an 1862 issue of the *Cincinnati Commercial,* an anglophone journalist described Cajuns in quite negative terms. The writer noted that a Cajun "is a half-savage creature, of mixed French and Indian blood. They live in the swamps, and subsist by fishing and hunting and cultivating a small patch of corn and sweet potatoes. They are sallow, dried-up and mummy-like in appearance, and stolid and stupid in expression." In another example, Henry noted that a writer in 1901 explained that Cajun conveys disdain. "It does not at all appear to be the abbreviated form of Acadian," the writer catalogued; "it is applied indiscriminately to any Creole who, whatever its origin, smells like the country and looks like a peasant."

Eventually, Cajun came to refer to any francophone or creolophone white who was low on the socioeconomic scale, even if they had no Acadian ancestry at all. At the turn of the twentieth century, Louisiana remained a region stricken with high rates of poverty—meaning there were plenty of people who fit into the evolving classification of Cajun. Often, anglophone outsiders documenting the region continued to enforce stereotypes of these Cajuns as a group of backward swamp dwellers. While not all historical references to Cajuns were inherently negative, Henry noted that calling someone a Cajun was often seen as an insult well into the twentieth century.

What helped to further bolster a Cajun identity linked to Acadian heritage was the handy work of Acadian "boosters" in the early part of the twentieth century who sought to highlight the Acadian influence in south Louisiana. State senator Dudley LeBlanc was one of the most well-known of them all. LeBlanc was a savvy businessman who became a millionaire by peddling his cure-all tonic Hadacol. He used his marketing wit to also promote Acadian ancestry. In 1930, LeBlanc and twenty-five "Evangeline Girls," evoking the Evangeline character from Henry Wadsworth Longfellow's 1847 epic poem, traveled to Nova Scotia to commemorate the 175th anniversary of the Acadians' expulsion from their homeland. This troop of women extolled the virtues of Acadian Louisiana while dressed in milkmaid costumes. The schtick was a hit. LeBlanc made connections with Acadians in Nova Scotia and New Brunswick that further fueled Louisianans' ties to their long-lost cousins. While those connections certainly existed, nearly two hundred years separated the Acadians of the North from those of the South—the latter group had long assimilated into Louisiana Creole culture. Even still, the Acadian narrative was an attractive one to the population of poor whites—a people expelled from their homeland who found refuge in Louisiana and, by the grace of their own hard work, built a unique culture. This, in a way, took the pejorative nature of the Cajun label and turned it into a badge of honor and prosperity. Cajuns weren't just poor francophones or creolophones, derided by their more affluent neighbors. Being Cajun was something to be proud of.

The Acadian connection only strengthened, and, in the late 1960s, as ethnic revival movements spread through the United States and Quebec, Canada, the people of Louisiana mounted their own effort. At the time, there were still an estimated one million francophones and creolophones in southern Louisiana, but the heritage languages had begun a steady decline among younger generations. Folks wanted to revive French and to preserve the culture of the region. The Council for the Development of French in Louisiana (CODOFIL) was created in 1968 to lead the charge in preserving the French language—essentially leaving out the Creole language despite a sizable population of native speakers. CODOFIL's rallying cry to describe Louisiana's francophone culture was characterized by the Cajun label with its roots in Acadia, and it began appearing like it never had before. As Trépanier noted, "The word Acadian became a synonym for Cajun, and was used as such. 'Acadian' and 'Acadia' sprang up all over the landscape in the names of businesses and festivals . . . Furthermore, in 1971, the state legislature chose the name 'Acadiana' to designate the culture area of Southern Louisiana. The flag that was going to fly over it was the 'Louisiana Acadian Flag.' This definition made awkward the place of Italian, Spanish, German, Scots-Irish 'Cajuns' by referring to an old Acadian identity, and definitely prevented blacks and Indians of French culture from being Cajuns."

The pervasiveness of the Cajun label has, in a way, rewritten history for many Louisianans. This has impacted how people see themselves and their past. Even in places with little Acadian settlement, people claim a Cajun heritage. Take Eunice, for example, which calls itself "Louisiana's Cajun Prairie Capital." As Alexandra Giancarlo pointed out in "'Don't Call Me a Cajun!': Race and Representation in Louisiana's Acadiana Region," around a third of the city is comprised of Black residents, and only about 14 percent of the population has Acadian surnames. Giancarlo noted that places like Lafayette and St. Landry Parish, thought of as Cajun Country, in fact have more Creole surnames than Acadian ones.

The term Cajun Country was used by the state tourism department in the 1990s in marketing campaigns that further bolstered the Acadian origins myth. Giancarlo wrote that the promotion of Cajun Country has covered up the true history of certain regions while changing how Louisianans perceive the origins of their traditions. This is evident in the "Cajun Mardi Gras" in Mamou, which has long been a favorite of national publications looking for a taste of Cajun culture. The late Anthony Bourdain visited Mamou's Mardi Gras in 2018 for an episode called "Cajun Mardi Gras" for the show *Parts Unknown* that aired on CNN. Giancarlo wrote that the Mamou celebration proclaims to offer "a taste of down-home, authentic Cajun life—never mind the inconvenient fact that most of the region's original families are French Creoles who immigrated from Alabama in the 1760s, not Acadia."

Shane K. Bernard, in his book *The Cajuns,* wrote that the region's many white ethnic groups turned into a single one, dubbed the Cajuns, which "ceased to describe a mainly French-speaking, non-materialistic, impoverished people on the fringe of American society and instead referred to a largely English-speaking, consumer-oriented, middle-class community whose members closely resembled mainstream Americans."

Contemporaneously with the Cajun pride movement, the local

civil rights movement was reaching its peak. While white scholars and activists rushed to define the Cajun community, Brasseaux noted, Creoles of color, "who at that time held a disproportionately large number of leadership positions in southern Louisiana Civil Rights organizations, continued to channel most of their energies into the cause of social and political equality until the late 1980s." They were, in many ways, left out of Louisiana's evolving cultural picture.

Since almost all Cajuns and Creoles are monolingual anglophones today, the terms no longer relate to language, Acadian ancestry, nativeness, or socioeconomic standing. Most people in Louisiana who identify as Cajun are white, and many Black Louisianans identify as Creole. Writing for *64 Parishes,* Giancarlo noted, "Today, it is reasonable to suggest that any Black person in south Louisiana could lay claim to the term Creole, and more often than not, it is used as a cultural signifier rather than a racial one. Ask ten self-identifying Creoles, and more than half will confirm that Creole is their ancestry, their heritage, or their culture; their race, however, is Black or African American." The same goes for south Louisiana's white population who typically identify as Cajun—their regional culture and francophone or creolophone heritage is what makes them Cajun, whether their ancestors were Acadian or not.

While Cajuns and Creoles share many cultural and regional practices, within these binary identity markers exist unique elements, notably due to the lived and ancestral experiences of each group. Within today's Creole culture, for example, there are traditions such as the trail rides of southwest Louisiana, where Black Creoles get together and ride horses through the countryside as a cultural gathering born out of a long history of horsemanship. According to Conni Castille, director of the documentary *T-Galop: A Louisiana Horse Story,* America's first cowboys were the Black Creoles of Louisiana. Meanwhile, in New Orleans, Creole culture can comprise Mardi Gras Indian celebrations, which feature Black Creoles donning elaborate costumes paying homage to the Native Americans who offered enslaved Africans refuge.

* * *

The Cajun obsession has also been featured prominently in Louisiana's culinary landscape. Often when discussing food in the state, it's described collectively as Cajun food. Lafayette's tourism website boasted that the city is "the epicenter of Cajun cuisine." Even New Orleans, which historically had few Acadian settlers, claimed on its tourism website to have Cajun food throughout the city.

Often, when discussing food and not ethnicity, the terms Cajun and Creole generally describe the foodways perfected two ways: Cajun food in the countryside that was made by Acadians, with the other being Creole by the people of New Orleans. This difference is said to be represented by the presence of tomatoes. "Creole cuisine uses tomatoes and proper Cajun food does not," noted Jay D. Ducote for Louisiana's official tourism website. Ducote went on to suggest that New Orleans Creole cuisine "is a blend of the various cultures of New Orleans including Italian, Spanish, African, German, Caribbean, Native American and Portuguese, to name a few. Creole cuisine is thought of as a little higher brow or aristocratic compared to Cajun." Ducote then asserted that the Acadians "were an extremely resourceful people who combined the flatlands, bayous, and wild game of South Louisiana with its proximity to the Gulf of Mexico to create a truly unique local cuisine. While many Acadiana residents today have African, Native American, German, French, or Italian roots, among others (which have all influenced Louisiana Cuisine in their own ways), their way of life is strongly influenced by the Cajun culture." This sounds awfully similar to Alan Lomax's soundbite about Cajun Country.

What emerges is a narrative that limits so-called Creole food to the New Orleans metro area, while the rest of south Louisiana's culinary landscape is the handiwork of the Acadians. Often, the Cajun label is attached to dishes or ingredients without Acadian origins, such as *maque choux* and tasso (Indigenous), jambalaya (Spanish Afro-Caribbean), andouille (German), and, at times, gumbo (African and Indigenous). In Thomas W. Anger's 1985 cookbook *Cajun Cuisine: Authentic Cajun Recipes from Louisiana's Bayou Country,* Marie Louise Comeaux Manuel credited the creation of gumbo to the Acadians who, "being conservative and possessing a great deal of ingenuity . . . concocted the delectable dish, gumbo." Manuel, who at the time was a retired director of the School of Home Economics at the University of Southwestern Louisiana (now ULL), equated Cajun cuisine to Acadian cooking.

Of course, gumbo was not created by the Acadians at all. The elements that led to the creation of gumbo were well established before the first group of Acadians stepped foot in Louisiana in 1764. In fact, most of the elements for the base of Louisiana's cuisine in general were well-established years before the arrival of the Acadians—a relatively small group who settled among tens of thousands of Creoles with an already established food culture. In *New Orleans*

Cuisine, Cynthia LeJeune Nobles wrote, "[Enslaved people] likely introduced the Acadians to okra. They also gave them hot spices, while the Native Americans introduced them to filé and herbs. The Germans of Louisiana's German Coast are generally credited with teaching the Acadians how to make sausage, especially andouille. The Native Americans taught their new neighbors how to make tasso." Nobles further pointed out that Haitians brought with them an affinity for hot spices and slow-cooking their food.

Acadian cuisine, never known for its use of spices like cayenne, centered around vegetables like cabbage. Around the time of the deportation in 1755, a favorite dish of the Acadians was *soupe de la toussaint,* a soup made with cabbage, turnips, and occasionally pork. The Acadians had to often boil their meals for hours, which could contain salt pork or old yard hens, in order to make the meat palatable. It's easy to see how their cooking methods lent to a quick adoption of the Louisiana gumbo, similarly cooked low and slow in a big cauldron. In 1804, Frenchman C. C. Robin noted the presence of gumbo at a *bal de maison,* or house dance, among a group of Acadians forty years after the first of them had arrived in Louisiana. This clearly displays that the Acadians were quick to absorb the regional cuisine of their neighbors.

Regionality has long shaped Louisiana cuisine in this way—people adopt the food of their neighbors. The so-called Cajun gumbo of southwest Louisiana—typically made with fowl and sausage—looks a bit different than its so-called New Orleans Creole counterpart with tomatoes more than one hundred miles away due to regional variation and minute differences in the area's food culture.

In the end, the ethnic labels often attached to gumbo—Creole or Cajun—do little to describe the endless variations of the dish. Gumbo is dynamic and doesn't fit neatly into one single category. Even neighbors can cook a different sort of gumbo. Sure, gumbo is the product of regionality, but also of personal preference, ingredient availability, and, likely, tradition—how Mom or Mawmaw taught you how to make it.

5

Gumbo's Future

It's nearly 80 degrees in mid-December, a few days before Christmas in the midst of a south Louisiana winter warm spell. I'm in a makeshift milking shed somewhere in the country near Duson, a small town just west of Lafayette, watching Stevie Mizzi as she coaxes milk from her dairy cow, Daisy. Mizzi's other animals sound off at our presence—ducks quacking in a nearby pond, cows mooing loudly as they shuffle to be next in the milking line, and pigs grunting with glee while they munch on pumpkins.

Looking after these animals while also raising three children on this rural homestead has demanded much of Mizzi's attention for a decade. Although she has a master's degree in psychology, she spends her time farming, growing, milking, slaughtering, and fermenting right from this patch of land in order to feed her kids and

Opposite: Stevie Mizzi's backyard homestead provides practically every ingredient that goes on the dinner table. It's this sort of existence that led to the evolution of Louisiana gumbo. (Photo by Sol Mizzi)

husband. The grocery store is always there if needed, but typically whatever goes on their table has been taken from right here in the backyard.

"When you're producing most of your food, you start to cook intuitively," she tells me, her hands squeezing milk into a tin bucket below Daisy. "I think people cook backwards these days where they think, 'Okay, what do I want to make? I want to make a gumbo. Okay, what are the ingredients I need? Let me go to the store and get it.' We cook the other way, which is, 'What do we have? Oh, great. We have everything for a gumbo. Let's make that.'"

This sort of seasonality played an important role in the development of gumbo. The various versions of the dish were birthed, in part, based on what was in season. Writing of seasonality, the authors of the *The Picayune's Creole Cook Book* noted that the "Creoles have an old adage that 'Nature itself tells us what to eat,' in the various vegetables and fruits of each season, and in the varieties of fish and flesh meat that are particularly adapted to each season." Okra, rice, and tomatoes, for instance, are harvested in the warmer months, making this combination ideal for a summer gumbo. As the Creole proverb suggests, seasonality extended to meat, too. In *The Omnivore's Dilemma: A Natural History of Four Meals,* Michael Pollan wrote that industrial farming methods have allowed a year-round supply of fresh meat, something that once was also at the whim of seasonality. "People would eat most of their beef and pork in the late fall or winter, when the animals were fat, and eat chicken in the summer." This would mean that chicken gumbos could be a summer option, while sausage or tasso might have appeared more in the winter when neighbors hosted a *boucherie,* or a communal pig butchering. Seafood like shrimp goes through estuarian cycles, moving from the Gulf of Mexico and the shallow marshes at certain times of the year, which made it available seasonally.

These rules even applied to people living in metropolitan areas. New Orleans's French Market has offered meats and vegetables since the late eighteenth century, when it was supported by a collection of small farmers, foragers, and fishermen. Groups of Choctaw sold locally harvested filé twice a week, for example, while the Germans just a few miles upriver provided seasonal grains and vegetables. For the Louisiana families outside of New Orleans, like where Mizzi lives, surviving meant reliance on vegetables from backyard gardens—things like turnips, mustard greens, potatoes, corn, and cabbage. Hunting and trapping provided deer, waterfowl, and small game like squirrels. What was caught, killed, or grew determined what went in the gumbo pot, to a large extent. But the community played a role just as crucial. Writing of the Cajuns in Louisiana, the authors of *Stir the Pot* noted that community bonds aided in all sorts of tasks, from building houses to feeding each other. Yet, as modernity reached small communities, these connections started to fray: "*Boucheries* satisfied the need for fresh provisions and social contact until the advent of refrigeration, which eventually phased out the need for communal butcheries."

If there is a downside to the way Mizzi lives, it's this lack of cultural cohesiveness. "I wish I didn't have to do all this," she tells me. "Just like my ancestors didn't have to do all of it. My grandpa said they had one dairy cow for the family who all kind of lived close by, the uncles and the grandparents and everybody, and they milked what they needed. And they had however many pigs to feed the whole extended family."

These days, the inconvenience of seasonality has been replaced by the expediency of the stocked grocery shelf. Therefore, Mizzi's lifestyle is considered by many of her neighbors as counterculture, different, even odd. She feels that too many Louisianans are content with creature comforts and eating like most Americans do. Instead of making gumbo like her great-grandparents, with an old yard hen that was boiled for hours to make a broth, the masses will opt for a store-bought stock with monosodium glutamate (MSG) as a flavor enhancer. These sorts of ingredients are replicas, Mizzi tells me, designed to mimic the robust flavors stewed up by her ancestors: "Modern-day Cajuns have never really tasted what gumbo is supposed to be, in my opinion."

Mizzi's gumbo embodies the laws of availability and seasonality. She grows her own meat chickens in a moveable coop just a few yards from where I'm standing. The sausage comes from pigs across a nearby fence, which are Kunekunes, a heritage breed that can be raised solely on pasture. Onions and garlic are plucked right from the soil in her nearby garden. So are bell peppers and cayenne peppers. Daisy's milk provides the cream to make butter, which Mizzi uses to make roux. What can't be grown on the farm Mizzi procures elsewhere, if possible. She'll catch shrimp and crabs on the coast in the spring and summer. Or hunt deer in the winter. The only gumbo ingredients Mizzi hasn't grown herself are rice and flour, although she's experimenting with cultivating both.

In Mizzi's eyes, today's Louisiana cuisine is a mirage of its former self, and it all comes down to the quality of the ingredients. What's a gumbo if it's stewed with MSG and meat pumped with antibiotics? "People are eating so much junk and so much tasteless food that they don't even know that the gumbo is tasteless or the filé is tasteless," she said. "Because we're used to that. Everything we buy in the store is not fresh. It's processed. It's got all these additives."

While shifting identity markers changed how Louisianans viewed themselves and their cuisine, the twentieth century also saw the reorganization of the nation's food system. Ingredients that were once seasonal are now available year-round at grocery stores thanks to industrial farming methods, which have influenced how gumbo is made—and tastes. These changes also transformed the way Louisianans interacted with food, marking a shift away from a connection to agricultural lifestyles and regional cuisine to one dominated by mainstream American food culture. From Mizzi's perspective, she surmises, "we've just lost all appreciation for food."

* * *

If you've eaten a chicken-and-sausage gumbo lately, chances are that the bird was a Cornish cross. This breed of broiler chicken, a bird produced strictly for meat, is a hybrid, a mix between the Cornish and the White Plymouth Rock. It was developed by Charles Vantress of California for the "Chicken of Tomorrow Contest" that the A&P Tea Company held in the 1940s and 1950s. Vantress's creation was deemed the best chicken to produce meat economically. The Cornish

cross was adopted by the meat industry in the 1950s, and today Big Poultry raises billions of them each year.

The Cornish cross isn't your run-of-the-mill chicken. In *The Omnivore's Dilemma,* Michael Pollan called them the "pinnacle of industrial chicken breeding." The birds are housed in warehouses the size of football fields—as many as twenty thousand can be crammed together. Due to this density, many farmers employ antibiotics to help quell disease. As an added bonus, the drugs speed up the rate at which the birds pack on pounds. It's not as if they need the help. Even without the medicine, Cornish crosses grow at a lightning pace. According to the Pacific Northwest Extension, a Cornish cross grows from near two ounces to more than six pounds in a mere six weeks—one chicken also consumes about ten pounds of feed. "It is the most efficient converter of corn into breast meat ever designed," Pollan wrote, "though this efficiency comes at a high physiological price: The birds grow so rapidly (reaching oven-roaster proportions in seven weeks) that their poor legs cannot keep pace, and frequently fail."

Even if a Cornish cross isn't sent to the slaughterhouse, it's unlikely to live very long before it succumbs to physical illness, a byproduct of the hybridization process. Often, Cornish crosses suffer heart attacks or other ailments throughout their short life spans as their muscle growth outpaces their organs. And even with the help of antibiotics, disease can run rampant in these CAFOs, or concentrated

Opposite: Stevie Mizzi holds up a recently butchered backyard chicken. Typically, her gumbos feature only what is grown and harvested from her land. (Photo by Kristen Soileau)

animal feeding operations. At the end of the day, the Cornish cross satiates America's desire for plump chickens in mere weeks—as a country, we eat about eight billion chickens a year.

It wasn't always this way. While today the average household consumes more than one hundred pounds of chicken each year, in 1970 it was closer to fifty. Before, it was even less—around ten pounds. That's because, before industrial farming, most chickens consumed by American families came, not from the grocery store, but from backyards in the form of roosters or old hens that had stopped laying eggs. In the twentieth century, America continued industrializing, expanding cities, growing its population. Megafarms began to replace smaller ones run by families. Chemicals that were the by-products of war led to the discovery of synthetic nitrogen. As Pollan put it, using synthetic fertilizer on farms "allowed the food chain to turn from the logic of biology and embrace the logic of industry. Instead of eating exclusively from the sun, humanity now began to sip petroleum."

Big Oil spurred changes in Louisiana, too. The discovery of petroleum along the state's coast led to a flood of English-speaking outsiders congregating in what was an isolated, predominantly francophone and creolophone region even at the beginning of the twentieth century. Jobs brought prosperity to many, but they required speaking English. Louisiana's 1921 state constitution essentially banned any language other than English in classrooms, accelerating a decline in the numbers of those who learned French or Creole as a first language. Americanization intensified as more highways linked together cities, war shipped farm boys across the world, and mass media like the radio and television brought mainstream American culture to

Cajun and Creole living rooms. The mechanization of farms sent Louisiana farmers, some of them still sharecroppers, looking for other jobs. According to the Census of Agriculture, in 1940, almost 7,000 Louisiana farms reported having a tractor. By 1950, that figure had jumped to more than 23,000. There were 170,216 farms in 1935 in Louisiana. In 1950, the number dropped to around 124,000, although the acreage farmed stayed relatively steady. Farms were getting bigger, and smaller operations were beginning to dwindle. Shane K. Bernard, in his book *The Cajuns,* wrote that Louisianans "gave up folk occupations to take better-paying blue-collar jobs in more urban settings, whether cities such as Lake Charles and Lafayette or smaller communities such as New Iberia, Morgan City, and Houma."

This move toward mainstream American culture eroded regional culture, morphing the area's population into another group of Anglo-Americans. These days, Bernard pointed out, Cajuns and Creoles engage in heritage practices as a sort of "symbolic ethnicity" that makes ethnic minorities "feel ethnic by participating in traditional holidays and festivals, by consuming traditional cuisine, and by listening to traditional music, among other activities—none of which require the burden of practicing folkways on a daily basis." Bernard noted that this symbolic ethnicity is on display in south Louisiana through "the consumption of ethnic cuisine, much of which is now available in the frozen food sections of supermarkets." In essence, ethnicity has become commercialized and centered on consumption, more of a pastime than an encompassing way of life.

This separation from the roots of cultural practices, including the ones that gave Louisiana its unique foodways, has severed the bond between people and traditions that are attached to the land. Wendell Berry, in his essay "The Pleasures of Eating," called this "cultural amnesia." Berry wrote that "when food, in the minds of eaters, is no longer associated with farming and with the land, then the eaters are suffering a kind of cultural amnesia that is misleading and dangerous." Berry concluded that the eater becomes a passive consumer, allowing capitalism to separate them from animals and plants. "And the result is a kind of solitude, unprecedented in human experience, in which the eater may think of eating as, first, a purely commercial transaction between him and a supplier and then as a purely appetitive transaction between him and his food."

The supplier that initiates this commercial transaction, or Big Ag, has touched every ingredient in the gumbo pot. Even though many local meat companies produce Louisiana sausage in-house, the pork was likely raised in a CAFO, the meat mixed with additives like MSG, sodium erythorbate, or hydrolyzed soy protein. Most filé looks and smells to be months old, comes from faraway forests, and is processed who-knows-how. Jarred roux often contains hydrogenated oil and highly processed flour. Any conventionally grown vegetables were cultivated with the help of chemical fertilizer and pesticides. As Berry wrote, "The business of the cosmeticians of advertising is to persuade the consumer that food so produced is good, tasty, healthful, and a guarantee of marital fidelity and long life." In Louisiana's case, foods are also marketed as authentically Cajun or Creole and made in a traditional way—ready-to-eat "authentic" gumbo in a box, for instance. Nothing about these industrial processes or the products they yield exudes tradition. Rather, traditional food items have been hijacked by the industrial system in order to produce a replica that comes packaged, labeled, and ready to eat. Whether many of us recognize it or not, as Berry noted, these factors actually form a wedge between people and tradition.

At almost every turn, the gumbo of today resembles a radically different dish from the one stewed up not so long ago. Although people feel connected culturally to gumbo, as a link to some sort of collective past, what the dish actually represents today is, in a way, disparate—its ingredients, the way it's discussed, and access to it aren't mirror images of the past. The people of south Louisiana are fundamentally different, too.

* * *

Mizzi and I walk to a parcel of land adjacent to her home. There's a pond here with open pasture, where her kids have free range to play. While we talk more about the food system, gumbo, the local culture, she keeps coming back to raising her kids. In essence, much of what she does is for them, their health, their future. When I tell her I believe she embodies the spirit that created Louisiana's regional cuisine, she smiles and shoots back that her lifestyle choice is simply an extension of motherhood. "And I think that that's how the women must have felt," she says, "when they were washing their dishes and cleaning their home and cooking their meals and growing their gardens and tending their animals. I think they were doing all of that for their family, to love their families, to take care of their husbands, to love their kids, to nourish them so they wouldn't get sick."

Ironically, it was this sort of wholesome vision that actually catapulted Louisiana cuisine to fame—thanks in large part to Paul Prudhomme, arguably one of the most well-known chefs of the twentieth century. One of thirteen children, Prudhomme was born in 1940 in Opelousas to poor sharecroppers. His mother, Hazel, taught him how to whip up simple country dishes using what they could raise on their farm. This upbringing stuck with him. Prudhomme told the *Nation's Restaurant News* in 2015 that when cooking potatoes at a restaurant in Colorado, he couldn't replicate the flavor of his mom's version. "So I decided to go back to a day in my life with Mom," Prudhomme said, "because when I helped her do these potatoes, they were wonderful. I wanted to see what she had done to them. And the most phenomenal thing happened; it changed my life. I remembered that the first thing we did was we went out into the field, and we dug them up."

This realization served as Prudhomme's inspiration, which guided him as a professional throughout his career. After working in kitchens and opening a few restaurants that fizzled, he found national fame in 1979 when he opened K-Paul's Louisiana Kitchen in New Orleans. Prudhomme prized fresh ingredients so much that his restaurant didn't have a freezer in it. K-Paul's offered the food he grew up with, like chicken and andouille gumbo thickened with a dark roux. His country-cooking influence spread as he garnered more national media attention, published cookbooks, and appeared on television shows. Prudhomme cooked for Presidents Ronald Reagan and Bill Clinton, and he dished up gumbo at the White House in 2007 for the annual Congressional Picnic.

Restaurants rode Prudhomme's wave of success. Those purporting to serve Cajun food began popping up in Los Angeles, New York

City, and Washington, but also in far-flung places like London and Bangkok. McDonald's featured Cajun chicken sandwiches. Pizza Hut had a "Traditional New Orleans–style Cajun Pizza." Weird creations like Cajun potato chips, Cajun French fries, or Cajun hamburgers began cropping up. However, these Cajun knock-off dishes missed the point of Prudhomme's approach—good Louisiana cooking comes from the freshest ingredients possible, not just a heavy supply of seasoning. The authors of *Stir the Pot* wrote that the "only link between corporate America's products and actual Cajun dishes was usually cayenne pepper."

As one of the first celebrity chefs in America, Prudhomme's popularity paved the way for others who are now household names. But his vision of Louisiana cuisine that's tied to quality ingredients also seemed to rub off on folks like Isaac Toups, owner of Toups' Meatery in New Orleans. Toups was born in Rayne, not far from Prudhomme's hometown in southwest Louisiana, where cooking and fresh ingredients were synonymous. "My dad makes one of the best gumbos on the planet," Toups told me, "because he uses wild ducks. And you can't get that if you don't know some Cajun dude with a shotgun. He puts the hearts and the gizzards and everything else in there." Toups's country upbringing has convinced him that the key to making good food is using the best ingredients he can find. At his restaurant, stocks are made in-house using quality chicken. Garlic is freshly diced. Seafood is local. "There's no replicating that," he contended.

Toups told me he values using the traditional cuisine he grew up with as a springboard for experimentation. His menu has local favorites like boudin and cracklings but also braised lamb neck, elk, and fine wine. "I use dark beer in my gumbo," he told me. "I use an excessive amount of garlic. I like different types of peppers. Sometimes I put some smoked poblano in my gumbo. Well, people say, 'That's not Cajun.' I don't care. It tastes good. So, what I say is, when you're making gumbo, try different stuff."

Other contemporary New Orleans chefs employ a similar approach, bending the rules and showcasing ethnic fusions that might ruffle the feathers of purists. Marcus Jacobs, a chef at Marjie's Grill, has served a Thai curry gumbo. At Turkey and the Wolf, owned by Mason Hereford, there has been a gumbo on the menu with ingredients like potato chips. Other gumbos in the Crescent City contain fermented black beans and lime leaf, which reflect the influence of the many Vietnamese and Chinese newcomers to the region. After all, gumbo has been born out of this sort of experimentation and the blending of varying ethnic groups.

While even purists can accept some experimentation, Louisianans seem to have their limits. In 2016, Disney posted a gumbo recipe on its website that it called "Tiana's Healthy Gumbo." This rendition featured some of the usual suspects like green bell peppers and okra but also unfamiliar ones like kale and quinoa. Louisianans responded on social media with fury, blasting Disney for dubbing this creation as a gumbo. Posts of the recipe on Facebook and Twitter were swiftly deleted, while the YouTube video was made private. In December 2022, NYT Cooking published a recipe for a vegetarian gumbo, with a corresponding tweet that read: "This meatless gumbo has a distinct Louisiana flavor, thanks to the roux, Creole seasoning and the 'holy trinity' of Creole cooking (onion, celery, bell pepper)." The recipe called for liquid smoke and lentils, and Louisianans weren't convinced. The state's governor, John Bel Edwards, retweeted the post in kind with the caption, "Bless their hearts." Twitter users blasted the recipe as an assault on Louisiana cuisine, resembling a bean soup but certainly not gumbo. Others pointed out that a quasi-vegetarian gumbo already exists, what's called *gombo z'herbes.* The Times Picayune/Nola.com ran an editorial in response to the recipe, titled "No Offense, New York Times, but We've Got the Gumbo Thing Covered," noting that "a great New York institution has committed a grave offense against the cuisine of our state."

Even Toups, who values experimentation in cooking, noted that tradition and quality ultimately serve as his guides in the kitchen. When he approaches preparing a meal, he'll often ask himself what someone from back home would do: "At every little increment, I try to make every little part better without deviating too far from the original recipe. And I think that will separate people from here on out. Constantly making the quality of the ingredients better will make the gumbo better. There's no reason to deviate too far from the actual recipe."

While gumbo has been influenced a lot by restaurants, chefs, and marketing, most Louisianans cook gumbo at home for their family or friends. The ingredients come from a variety of places—the grocery store, farmers markets, from the swamps and woods, or right from the backyard. Gumbo is regional, can be seasonal or not, the product of tradition or experimentation. Some call it Cajun, others Creole, but either way, gumbo still serves the same purpose of bringing folks together at the dinner table.

So, while contemporary gumbo might be different in many ways, the dish still embodies the spirit of diversity of all the gumbos that came before. It's this diversity that makes gumbo so special. From West African okra stew to Choctaw soup to Creole gumbo to a favorite known around the world. It's unclear where the soup will evolve from here, but whatever it might be, with a Louisianan at the helm it's likely to taste good.

bibliography

Online Sources

Acadian Museum. "70th Anniversary of the 15 Young Evangeline Girls Who Came to Louisiana in 1946 for an Event-Filled 37-Day Trip." https://www.acadianmuseum.com/70th_anniversary.html.

Albert, Nico. "Food, Culture, and Storytelling." *PBS* (blog), November 8, 2018. https://www.pbs.org/native-america/blogs/native-voices/food-culture-and-storytelling/.

American Heritage Vegetables. "Okra." http://www.digitalussouth.org/vegetable/vegetable.php?vegName=Okra.

Bellarmine University. "Sassafras." https://www.bellarmine.edu/faculty/drobinson/sassafras.asp.

Bernard, Shane K. "Gumbo in 1764?" *Bayou Teche Dispatches* (blog), October 3, 2011. http://bayoutechedispatches.blogspot.com/2011/10/gumbo-in-1764.html

——. "Notes on the Birth of Cajun Ethnic Identity." *Bayou Teche Dispatches* (blog), February 12, 2022. https://bayoutechedispatches.blogspot.com/2020/09/notes-on-birth-of-cajun-ethnic-identity.html.

——. "On That Word 'Gumbo': Okra, Sassafras, and Baudry's Reports from 1802–1803." *Bayou Teche Dispatches* (blog), October 19, 2011. http://bayoutechedispatches.blogspot.com/2011/10/more-on-that-word-gumbo-okra-sassafras.html.

Cajun Country. Directed by Alan Lomax. Association for Cultural Equity, 1991. Folk Streams, https://www.folkstreams.net/films/cajun-country.

"Cajun or Creole: What's the Difference?" https://www.neworleans.com/restaurants/where-to-eat/cajun-or-creole/.

Certified Louisiana. https://certifiedlouisiana.org/.

"Chahta-ima." *New Orleans Bulletin,* August 10, 1875. Chronicling America: Historic American Newspapers. Library of Congress. https://chroniclingamerica.loc.gov/lccn/sn86079018/1875-08-10/ed-1/seq-1/.

Coder, Kim D. "Redbay (Persea borbonia): Drifting toward Oblivion." https://bugwoodcloud.org/resource/files/15175.pdf.

"The Creole Defined." *New Orleans Bulletin,* August 1, 1875. Chronicling America: Historic American Newspapers. Library of Congress. https://chroniclingamerica.loc.gov/lccn/sn86079018/1875-08-01/ed-1/seq-6/.

Dimitry, Alexander. "Gombo." *Le Meschacébé,* July 19, 1873. Chronicling America: Historic American Newspapers. Library of Congress. https://chroniclingamerica.loc.gov/lccn/sn86079080/1873-07-19/ed-1/seq-4/.

Dominican University Rebecca Crown Library. "Choctaw." https://research.dom.edu/NativeAmericanStudies/choctaw.

Ducote, Jay D. "Cajun vs. Creole Food—What's the Difference?" Louisiana Travel. https://www.louisianatravel.com/articles/cajun-vs-creole-food-what-difference.

Edwards, John Bel [@LouisianaGov]. "Bless Their Hearts." *Twitter,* December 16, 2022. https://twitter.com/LouisianaGov/status/1604207908329234433?cxt=HHwWgoCxnfulpcMsAAAA.

Elie, Lolis Eric. "The Afterlives of 'Creole Feast.'" *Bitter Southerner,* June 24, 2021.

"Gombo File." *Le Sentinelle de Thibodaux,* April 24, 1897. Chronicling America: Historic American Newspapers. Library of Congress. https://chroniclingamerica.loc.gov/lccn/sn88064492/1897-04-24/ed-2/seq-1/.

Griggs, Margene M. "Sassafras." https://www.srs.fs.usda.gov/pubs/misc/ag_654/volume_2/sassafras/albidum.htm.

Hermes, James. "Feeding Meat-type Chickens." March 2014. https://catalog.extension.oregonstate.edu/sites/catalog/files/project/pdf/pnw658.pdf.

The Historic Marker Database. "Thomas H Davis." https://www.hmdb.org/m.asp?m=49358.

The Historic New Orleans Collection. "German Settlers in Louisiana and New Orleans." https://www.hnoc.org/research/german-settlers-louisiana-and-new-orleans.

Hotard, Corey David, "Just Throw it in the Pot! The Cultural Geography of Hidden

Landscapes and Masked Performances in South Louisiana Gumbo Cooking." PhD diss., Louisiana State University, 2015. https://digitalcommons.lsu.edu/gradschool_dissertations/1493.

Hyatt, Phil. "Story of Kisatchie Botany." https://www.fs.usda.gov/detail/kisatchie/landmanagement/resourcemanagement/?cid=fsbdev3_024695.

"Isle Brevelle." *Louisiana Populist,* February 26, 1897. Chronicling America: Historic American Newspapers. Library of Congress. https://chroniclingamerica.loc.gov/lccn/sn88071004/1897-02-26/ed-1/seq-2/.

Lafayette Travel. "Welcome to Lafayette, Louisiana." https://www.lafayettetravel.com/.

Lee, Chan, "A Culture History of Rice with Special Reference to Louisiana." PhD diss., Louisiana State University, 1960. https://digitalcommons.lsu.edu/gradschool_disstheses/597.

"The Legacy of Slavery in the Caribbean and the Journey towards Justice." *UN Chronicle* (blog), March 24, 2022. https://www.un.org/en/un-chronicle/legacy-slavery-caribbean-and-journey-towards-justice.

Linscombe, Steven. "The History of U.S. Rice Production–Part 1." *LSU Ag Center Publications* (blog), December 8, 2006. https://www.lsuagcenter.com/portals/our_offices/research_stations/rice/features/publications/the-history-of-us-rice-production--part-1.

Lorell, Clair. "The New York Times Posts Vegetarian Gumbo Recipe, Gets Roasted." *Eater New Orleans* (blog), December 16, 2022. https://nola.eater.com/2022/12/16/23511482/new-york-times-posts-meatless-gumbo-recipe-gets-roasted.

"The Magic of Chef Paul-Making a Roux." YouTube, uploaded by Chef Paul Prudhomme's Magic Seasoning Blends, July 21, 2008. https://www.youtube.com/watch?v=Np3uGcdQNUw.

Miglore, Kristen. "Better, Lazier Gumbo Thanks to a Hands-off Roux." Food52, February 11, 2015.

Monteleone, Diana C. "German-Americans." Center for Louisiana Studies. https://cls.louisiana.edu/programming-special-projects/louisiana-101/peoples-places/german-americans.

Moss, Robert. "The Real Story of Gumbo, Okra, and Filé." *Serious Eats* (blog), August 10, 2018. https://www.seriouseats.com/history-new-orleans-gumbo-okra-file-powder.

National Toxicology Program, Department of Health and Human Services. "Safrole." *Report on Carcinogens,* no. 15 (2021). https://ntp.niehs.nih.gov/ntp/roc/content/profiles/safrole.pdf.

Newhall, David S. "Native Americans, Relations with French." In *Mississippi Encyclopedia,* February 2, 2018. https://mississippiencyclopedia.org/entries/native-americans-relations-with-french/.

"No Offense, New York Times, but We've Got the Gumbo Thing Covered." The Times Picayune/Nola.com, December 28, 2022. https://www.nola.com/opinions/our_views/our-views-we-dont-need-advice-from-ny-about-gumbo/article_bac59e92-813d-11ed-87e5-3b9f63bab269.html.

Olivier, Jonathan. "The Pot Thickens." *Bitter Southerner,* August 24, 2021.

Orr, Amos. "How to Make a Roux." *Visit Lake Charles* (blog), August 28, 2018. https://www.visitlakecharles.org/blog/post/how-to-make-a-roux/.

Piper, Kelsey. "How Chickens Took over America's Dinner Plates, in One Chart." *Vox,* February 19, 2021.

St. Landry Parish Tourist Commission. "It's Gumbo for Your Soul." https://www.cajuntravel.com.

St. Landry Whig, July 31, 1845. Chronicling America: Historic American Newspapers. Library of Congress. https://chroniclingamerica.loc.gov/lccn/sn83016702/1845-07-31/ed-1/seq-1/.

Strapagiel, Lauren. "Disney Removed a Recipe for 'Healthy' Gumbo after Southerners Called Them Out." *Buzz Feed News* (blog), September 14, 2016. https://www.buzzfeednews.com/article/laurenstrapagiel/shouldve-just-called-it-soup.

T-Galop: A Louisiana Horse Story. Directed by Conni Castille. Louisiana Public Broadcasting, 2021. YouTube. https://www.youtube.com/watch?v=eO-2xoSHJ50.

"That Mobile Coast." *Morning Star and Catholic Messenger,* November 25, 1877. Chronicling America: Historic American Newspapers. Library of Congress, https://chroniclingamerica.loc.gov/lccn/sn86086284/1877-11-25/ed-1/seq-4/.

Thorn, Bret. "Paul Prudhomme: A Remembrance." *Nation's Restaurant News* (blog), October 8, 2015. https://www.nrn.com/blog/paul-prudhomme-remembrance.

Twitty, Michael W. "The Secret History of Okra—Okra Soup." *Tori Avery* (blog), November 10, 2021. https://toriavey.com/history-okra-soup-recipe/.

US Department of Agriculture. "Census of Agriculture Historical Archive." https://agcensus.library.cornell.edu/census_parts/1950-louisiana/.

US Food & Drug Administration. "CFR—Code of Federal Regulations Title 21." https://www.accessdata.fda.gov/scripts/cdrh/cfdocs/cfcfr/cfrsearch.cfm?fr=189.180.

US Forest Service. "Silviculture and Timber." https://www.fs.usda.gov/detail/kisatchie/landmanagement/resourcemanagement/?cid=fsbdev3_024690.

Printed Sources

Ancelet, Barry. "Negotiating the Mainstream: The Creoles and Cajuns in Louisiana." *French Review* 80, no. 6 (2007): 1235–55.

Anderson, Brett. "Gumbo, the Classic New Orleans Dish, Is Dead: Long Live Gumbo." *New York Times,* January 8, 2019.

Angers, Thomas W. *Cajun Cuisine: Authentic Cajun Recipes from Louisiana's Bayou Country.* Lafayette, LA: Beau Bayou, 1985.

Bernard, Shane K. *The Cajuns: Americanization of a People.* Jackson: University Press of Mississippi, 2003.

Berry, Wendell. "The Pleasures of Eating." In *Bringing It to the Table: On Farming and Food,* 215–21. New York: Counterpoint, 2009.

Bienvenu, Marcelle, Carl A. Brasseaux, and Ryan A. Brasseaux. *Stir the Pot: The History of Cajun Cuisine.* New York: Hippocrene, 2005.

Brasseaux, Carl A. *French, Cajun, Creole, Houma: A Primer on Francophone Louisiana.* Baton Rouge: Louisiana State University Press, 2005.

Bushnell, David Ives. *The Choctaw of Bayou Lacomb, St. Tammany Parish, Louisiana.* Washington, DC: Government Printing Office, 1909.

Cathey, David. *A Culinary History of Pittsburg County: Little Italy, Choctaw Beer and Lamb Fries.* Charleston, SC: American Palate, 2013.

Christian Woman's Exchange. *The Creole Cookery Book.* New Orleans: T. H. Thomason, 1885.

Dethloff, Henry C. "Rice Revolution in the Southwest, 1880–1910." *Arkansas Historical Quarterly* 29, no. 1 (1970): 66–75.

Ellis, Elizabeth. "Houma Nation." *64 Parishes,* April 5, 2013.

Ellzey, Bill. "Taso Was a Tradition for Area Indian Families." *Houma Courier,* February 17, 2016.

Fessenden, Thomas Greene. *The New England Farmer.* Boston: Thomas W. Shepard, 1831.

Fisher, Abby. *What Mrs. Fisher Knows about Southern Cooking.* San Francisco: Women's Co-operative Printing Office, 1881.

Giancarlo, Alexandra. "'Don't Call Me a Cajun!': Race and Representation in Louisiana's Acadiana Region." *Journal of Cultural Geography* 36, no. 1 (2018): 23–48.

———. "Riders." *64 Parishes,* 2017.

Grimes, William. "Paul Prudhomme, Chef Who Put Cajun Cooking on National Stage, Dies at 75." *New York Times,* October 8, 2015.

Hall, Gwendolyn Midlo. *Africans in Colonial Louisiana: The Development of Afro-Creole Culture in the Eighteenth Century.* Baton Rouge: Louisiana State University Press, 1995.

Harris, Jessica B. *Iron Pots and Wooden Spoons: Africa's Gifts to New World Cooking.* New York: Atheneum, 1989.

———. "On Okra." *64 Parishes,* Fall 2007.

Hearn, Lafcadio. *La Cuisine Creole.* New Orleans: F. F. Hansell & Bro., 1885.

Henry, Jacques. "From 'Acadien' to 'Cajun' to 'Cadien': Ethnic Labelization and Construction of Identity." *Journal of American Ethnic History* 17, no. 4 (1998): 29–62.

Klingler, Thomas A. "How Much Acadian Is There in Cajun?" In *Acadians and Cajuns: The Politics and Culture of French Minorities in North America,* edited by Ursula Mathis-Moser and Gunter Bischof, 91–103. Innsbruck, Austria: Innsbruck University Press, 2009.

Lamont, William James. "Okra—A Versatile Vegetable Crop." *Hort Technology* 9, no. 2 (1999): 179–84.

Laudun, John. "Gumbo This: The State of a Dish." In *Acadians and Cajuns: The Politics and Culture of French Minorities in North America,* edited by Ursula Mathis-Moser and Gunter Bischof, 155–66. Innsbruck, Austria: Innsbruck University Press, 2009.

Leslie, Eliza. *Directions for Cookery, in Its Various Branches.* Philadelphia: Carey & Hart, 1840.

———. *Miss Leslie's New Cookery Book.* Philadelphia: T. B. Peterson & Bros., 1857.

Lombard, Rudy, and Nathaniel Burton. *Creole Feast: 15 Master Chefs of New Orleans Reveal Their Secrets.* New York: Random House, 1978.

Nobles, Cynthia L. "Gumbo." In *New Orleans Cuisine: Fourteen Signature Dishes and Their Histories,* edited by Susan Tucker, 98–115. Jackson: University Press of Mississippi, 2009.

Nosrat, Samin. "A Dish That Reflects Our Nation: Okra Soup." *New York Times,* September 22, 2020.

Pollan, Michael. *In Defense of Food: An Eater's Manifesto.* New York: Penguin, 2009.

——. *The Omnivore's Dilemma: A Natural History of Four Meals.* New York: Penguin, 2007.

Randolph, Mary. *The Virginia House-wife.* Washington, DC: Davis and Force, 1824.

Rothman, Joshua D. "Before the Civil War, New Orleans Was the Center of the U.S. Slave Trade." *Smithsonian Magazine,* April 19, 2021.

Rutledge, Sarah. *The Carolina Housewife.* Charleston, SC: W. R. Babcock, 1847.

Sloane, Eric. *A Reverence for Wood.* New York: Funk & Wagnalls, 1984.

Smith, Chris. *The Whole Okra: A Seed to Stem Celebration.* White River Junction, VT: Chelsea Green, 2019.

Stahls, Paul F. "Roux the Day." *Acadiana Profile,* January 1, 2010.

Steager, Tabitha Y. "Paul Prudhomme." In *Icons of American Cooking,* edited by Victor W. Geraci and Elizabeth S. Demers, 195–204. Santa Barbara, CA: ABC-CLIO & Greenwood, 2011.

——. *The Picayune's Creole Cook Book.* New Orleans: The Picayune, 1910.

Trépanier, Cécyle. "The Cajunization of French Louisiana." *Geographical Journal* 157, no. 2 (1991): 161–71.

Valdman, Albert, et al. *Dictionary of Louisiana French: As Spoken in Cajun, Creole, and American Indian Communities.* Jackson: University Press of Mississippi, 2009.

Warren, Gina G. *Hatched: Dispatches from the Backyard Chicken Movement.* Seattle: University of Washington Press, 2021.

Wells, Ken. *Gumbo Life: Tales from the Roux Bayou.* New York: Norton, 2019.

Wyatt, Megan. "Why Do Some People Put Tomatoes in Their Gumbo? Curious Louisiana Investigates." *Advocate,* August 28, 2022.

Zielinski, Sarah. "Stone Age Stew? Soup Making May Be Older Than We'd Thought." NPR, February 6, 2013.

Personal Interviews (conducted by the author)

Bernard, Shane K. May 31, 2021.

Elie, Lolis Eric. December 9, 2022.

Fuqua, Dusty. June 5, 2022.

Luster, Janie. December 15, 2022.

Mizzi, Stevie. December 12, 2022.

Toups, Isaac. November 10, 2022.

Twitty, Michael. November 15, 2022.